Also from Gi.. .....

Making the Choice
When Typical School Doesn't Fit Your Atypical Child

Forging Paths
Beyond Traditional Schooling

If This is a Gift, Can I Send it Back?
Surviving in the Land of the Gifted and Twice Exceptional

Learning in the 21st Century
How to Connect, Collaborate, and Create

How to Work and Homeschool
Practical Tips, Advice, and Strategies from Parents

Educating Your Gifted Child
How One Public School Teacher Embraced Homeschooling

Self-Directed Learning
Documentation and Life Stories

Gifted, Bullied, Resilient
A Brief Guide for Smart Families

Writing Your Own Script
A Parent's Role in the Gifted Child's Social Development

Micro-Schools
Creating Personalized Learning on a Budget

●

Coming Soon from GHF Press

Kelly Hirt
Twelve Ways to Lift Up Our Twice-Exceptional Children

Amy Harrington
Radical Unschooling

Kathleen Humble
Gifted Myths

Lori Dunlap
A Guide for College Admissions Professionals

Your Rainforest Mind
A Guide to the Well-Being of Gifted Adults and Youth

By Paula Prober

Published by GHF Press

A Division of Gifted Homeschoolers Forum

3701 Pacific Ave. SE - PMB #609

Olympia, WA 98501

ISBN-13: 978-0692713105 (GHF Press)

ISBN-10: 0692713107

Cover design by Shawn Keehne

www.shawnkeehne.com • skeehne@mac.com

To all of the rainforest-minded souls. May you live like the thriving rain forest—in peace, grace, balance and beauty and in support of all beings on the planet.

Contents

Introduction ix

Do You Have a Rainforest Mind? xv

Chapter One
    Too Much: Intensity, Sensitivity, Empathy 17

Chapter Two
    If You're So Smart, Why Aren't You Saving the World? 37

Chapter Three
    Perfectionism, Precision, Procrastination 53

Chapter Four
    Too Many Possibilities, Too Many Choices 81

Chapter Five
    Going It Alone 105

Chapter Six
    School Daze 121

Chapter Seven
    Authenticity and Creativity and Spirituality, Oh My! 139

Chapter Eight
    Stop the Deforestation 159

Crystalline Structures 163

Recommended Resources 167

Endnotes 175

Index 183

Acknowledgments 191

About the Author 193

Introduction

[I]t probably doesn't matter if we try too hard, are awkward sometimes, care for one another too deeply, are excessively curious about nature, are too open to experience, enjoy a nonstop expense of the senses in an effort to know life intimately and lovingly. It probably doesn't matter if, while trying to be modest and eager watchers of life's many spectacles, we sometimes look clumsy or get dirty or ask stupid questions or reveal our ignorance or say the wrong thing or light up with wonder like the children we all are. It probably doesn't matter if a passerby sees us dipping a finger into the moist pouches of dozens of lady slippers to find out what bugs tend to fall into them, and thinks us a bit eccentric. Or a neighbor, fetching her mail, sees us standing in the cold with our own letters in one hand and a seismically red autumn leaf in the other, its color hitting our senses like a blow from a stun gun, as we stand with a huge grin, too paralyzed by the intricately veined gaudiness of the leaf to move.

~Diane Ackerman, *A Natural History of the Senses*[1]

In the following pages, you will meet excessively curious, idealistic, sensitive, highly intelligent humans—individuals with rainforest minds (RFM). You will meet Billy, an adolescent with extraordinary empathy for all beings and a deep desire for precision, ethics, and excellence. His multiple sensitivities and his complicated perfectionism were misunderstood by teachers, peers, family, and himself. As a result, he felt that something was terribly wrong with him, nothing he did was ever good enough. You will also get to know Gina, a twenty-something grad student whose brain ran faster, wider, and deeper than many of her university professors. She overwhelmed and alienated her less effervescent peers, so Gina watched TV and smoked pot to find comfort, procrastinate, and feel normal.

You will meet Gwen, who at 52 completed an interdisciplinary PhD in anthropology, history, art, and feminism. Lonely since childhood, she had an early awareness of human suffering. Her lifetime of divergent interests led her into many endeavors but she had yet to find a partner who matched her intellect or emotional range. You will also meet Steven, a 35-year-old single parent who was deeply troubled by his difficulty controlling his anger at his son, Tim. Steven expressed frustration with educators when Tim was acting out in school and feared that he would repeat the patterns of his abusive alcoholic father. Steven longed to find ways to heal his family's legacy and access the creative and spiritual spark within his heart.

In this book, you will meet these and other RFM clients with whom I have worked in my counseling practice over the last 25 years. Some entered therapy to examine the roots of their depression, despair, or anxiety. Others wanted to understand their frustrations with relationships, schooling, or career paths. Many experienced trauma in childhood. All of them felt the pressures, pleasures, and peculiarities of living inside the highly intense and complicated rainforest mind.

These clients did not come to me because they identified themselves as gifted. RFM adults generally seek counseling for the same reasons most people do. The difference is that, because of their rainforest characteristics, they experience extra layers of complexity. Understanding and unraveling these layers helps them learn how to thrive in a seemingly alien world. Contrary to the mythology that "smart" people will be just fine without help, what often comes with smart is excessive doubt, anxiety, depression, shame, and loneliness.[2]

I hope to help you (and your partners, relatives, friends, psychotherapists, and educators) make sense out of your jungle of thoughts, emotions, sensitivities, questions, dreams, worries, obsessions, intuitions, joys, disillusionments, fears, insights, curiosities, rages, expectations, ideals, high standards, failures, and successes. As you better understand the workings of your rainforest mind, you can find greater purpose, meaning, and direction. With a clearer sense of your true self, you can live like the thriving rain forest—in balance, peace, grace, and beauty, and in support of all beings on the planet.

What is a Rainforest Mind?

If you think of people as ecosystems, you can see some as meadows, others as deserts, some as mountains—and some as rain forests. While all ecosystems are beautiful and make valuable contributions to the whole, rain forests are particularly complex: multi-layered, highly sensitive, colorful, intense, creative, fragile, overwhelming, and misunderstood, while thick with possibility and pulsing with life, death, and transformation. You could say that a rain forest has far more activity than, say, a meadow or a wheat field. The rain forest is not a better ecosystem, just more complicated. It also makes an essential contribution to the planet when allowed to be itself, rather than when cut down and turned into something that it is not.

The term "rainforest mind" covers more than just thinking, cognition, or brain. It includes heart, soul, body, and spirit.

You may have noticed that the book's title includes the word "gifted." This is where it can get awkward. Perhaps you have never described yourself as gifted. You are not Einstein nor have you won a Nobel Prize. But, in my experience, giftedness is not only mental acuity or cognitive ability. It is not only about achievement. In my counseling practice and in the literature which I will refer to, giftedness is defined as a set of characteristics, including sensitivity, empathy, and perfectionism. It may or may not include high grades, achievement, or eminence. Great accomplishments may occur, but not necessarily. After all, the rain forest achieves by simply being itself. Certainly, much controversy surrounds "giftedness," and different types of giftedness exist.[3] I shall be presenting my version and you can decide if it works for you.

Social-Emotional-Spiritual Issues

People with rainforest minds have particular characteristics that might confuse and overwhelm them and their family, friends, teachers, and therapists. In my work with RFMs in schools and in my counseling practice, I have found them to be incredibly diverse. Even so, they often have certain social, emotional, and, at times, spiritual issues in common that can make life challenging, weird, miraculous, lonely, depressing, and fascinating.[4] These concerns, and what to do about them, will be the focus of this book.

All of my client cases are used with permission. Names and physical descriptions are changed to maintain anonymity, and many cases have been simplified to protect client privacy. While therapy is usually multi-dimensional, for this book, I highlighted the moments that focused on the issues most related to their rainforest mind. And, as is typical, many of these clients will be doing various forms of inner work throughout their lives.

I tried to make each case study fit neatly within its appropriate chapter. I was unsuccessful. Instead, you will notice some emphasis on the issue described in the chapter followed by a broader description of the client and a more holistic presentation of the case. Just like the rain forest, these individuals have too many vines curling every which way to stuff them into a single chapter's topic. Thank you in advance for understanding.

I admit up front that I live in a very homogeneous part of Oregon where the populations of people of color are limited. Thus, my examples do not reflect the wide range of RFMs from diverse groups as much as I would have liked.

The following chapters reflect my personal, anecdotal perspective on giftedness in adults and teens based on my experience in the field beginning in the mid-1970s. I expect that you will be analytical, questioning, and skeptical, as is your nature.

My Story

My trek into the rainforest mind began in 1973 when I graduated from college and became a sixth-grade teacher in a junior high school in Wilmington, Delaware. Very early in my career, two of my colleagues commented that my teaching style matched what gifted children needed to thrive in school.

My response was, "What's a gifted child?" I was intrigued and decided to find out.

Soon after, I landed a job teaching gifted middle school students in Pennsylvania in a "pull-out program." Identified gifted students left their regular classrooms for two and a half hours a week to join their peers in a class with me. They explored topics of interest in greater depth and at a faster pace than the regular classroom allowed. They met peers with whom they could form deep friendships. I fell in love with these kids' curious, analytical, energetic, funny, questioning, intense, eccentric, creative, sensitive, emotional, quirky, perceptive, intuitive, obsessive, precocious selves. I had found my niche.

When I was about to turn 30, I felt drawn to leave central Pennsylvania to find a more progressive environment. I settled into Eugene, Oregon's organic tofu culture and was able to continue working with gifted children in grades one through five. Gradually, through the University of Oregon, Pacific University, and Oregon State University, I expanded my work to include classes for educators on how to teach gifted children in the regular classroom, and I presented workshops for parents.

At age 39, I enrolled in a master's degree program in counseling. It was time to leave the field of education for the mental health world. I had been a client in psychotherapy for a few years and loved the deep introspective process and the growth, change, and healing that resulted. Upon graduation, I worked in a mental health agency for four years and then started a private practice.

Soon after, it occurred to me that I could specialize in counseling gifted adults and consulting with parents of gifted children. I had learned that they had particular mental health needs and I believed that my experience and awareness of the issues could make a difference. Sometime during that period, I also developed the "rainforest mind" concept. I needed some way to help people understand this population without using the controversial "g" word. In March 2014, I started blogging about gifted adults and about parenting gifted children.

And so, for the past 30+ years, I have had the honor and privilege of exploring the deep, lush, vivid terrain of rainforest-minded souls.

Do You Have a Rainforest Mind?

Take the following highly unscientific quiz to find out.

1. Like the rain forest, are you intense, multilayered, colorful, creative, overwhelming, highly sensitive, complex, idealistic, and influential?
2. Are you misunderstood, misdiagnosed, and mysterious?
3. Like the rain forest, have you met too many chainsaws?
4. Do people tell you to lighten up when you are just trying to enlighten them?
5. Are you overwhelmed by breathtaking sunsets, itchy clothes, strong perfumes, clashing colors, bad architecture, buzzing that no one else hears, angry strangers, needy friends, or global hunger?
6. Do you see ecru, beige, and sand where others see only white?
7. Do you spend hours looking for the exact word, precise flavor, smoothest texture, right note, perfect gift, finest color, most meaningful discussion, fairest solution, or deepest connection?
8. Have you ever called yourself ADHD because you are easily distracted by new ideas or intricate cobwebs, or OCD because you alphabetize your home library or color-code your sweaters, or bipolar because you go from ecstasy to despair in 10 minutes?
9. Are you passionate about learning, reading, and research, yet perplexed, perturbed, and perspiring about schooling?
10. Do your intuition and empathy tell you what family members, neighbors, and stray dogs think, feel, or need even before they know what they think, feel, or need?
11. Do you find decision-making about your future career and deciding what color to paint the bedroom equally daunting due to the deluge of possibilities assaulting your frontal lobes?
12. Are your favorite spiritual conversations the ones you have with trees, rocks, and babbling brooks?
13. Does your worth depend on your achievements, so that if you make a mistake or do not perform up to your standards, you feel like an utter failure as a human being now and forever more?

14. Do you crave intellectual stimulation and are you desperate to find even one person who is fascinated by fractals or thrilled by theology?

15. Are you embarrassed to tell your family and friends that you find it easier to fall in love with ideas than with people?

16. Have you ruminated about the purpose of life and your contribution to the betterment of humanity since you were young?

17. Do you get blank, confused stares from people when you think you have just said something really funny?

18. Are people awestruck at what you can accomplish in a day, but if they knew the real you, they would see that you are actually a lazy, procrastinating, slacking impostor?

19. Are you afraid of: failure/success, losing/winning, criticism/praise, mediocrity/excellence, stagnation/change, not fitting in/fitting in, low expectations/high expectations, boredom/intellectual challenge, not being normal/being normal?

20. Do you long to drive a Ferrari at top speed on the open road, but find yourself always stuck on the freeway in L.A. during rush hour?

21. Do you love skipping down new sensual paths and exploring imaginary worlds to discover beautiful connections between fascinating objects, words, ideas, or images?

22. Do you wonder how you can feel like "not enough" and "too much" at the same time?

23. Are you uncomfortable with the label "gifted," and sure that if you were to use the word as a descriptor of people with some sort of advanced intelligence—which you would not because it is so offensive—that it certainly would not apply to you?

If you answered "yes" to at least 12 of the above questions, you likely have a rainforest mind. If you ruminated about the answers to many of these questions and often thought "it depends," you, too, fit the profile.

Chapter One

Too Much: Intensity, Sensitivity, Empathy

Many gifted adults describe their nervous systems in terms of a built-in antenna device that seems to reach as high as radar and as deep as sonar. Some report experiences of being tremendously absorbent, taking in life experiences through their pores like a sponge . . . The pressure to respond to the slightest shift in barometric pressure, a bright light or loud noise, a pungent aroma, commotion or emotional upheaval, or tiny blips in the way their body is working, can make the life of a gifted adult a rich tapestry of experience. It can also wear them out.
~Mary-Elaine Jacobsen[5]

A Lush Landscape

Typically, the world of the rainforest mind is very intense. For example, you are likely to think a lot and very quickly, on more than one track at a time, sometimes in random directions. And, as if that were not enough, you probably have deep complex emotions that could spill out over the furniture and run down the walls if you let them, which you probably do not, especially if you are a male.[6] Regardless, you are probably still capable of feeling both despair and delight within, say, a 30-minute period. This can be uncomfortable, embarrassing, and, to others, diagnosable.[7] You may live in a rich imaginative passionate inner world that you can only describe in poetry, dance, music, or mathematical equations.[8] This intensity is often internalized and may not be recognized by others, or even by you, for what it is.

Another way to say this is that your perception, awareness, and sensitivities are turned up high. This can apply to sounds, textures, smells, chemicals, tastes, colors, images, and air quality. You may hear sounds that others miss or not be able to wear particular clothes due to their texture. You may have to avoid certain movies because of disturbing images. If you take medications, you may have to take smaller amounts than most people.[9] You likely perceive things that others do not, and have insights that are obvious to you but not apparent to those around you. This combination of awareness and sensitivity can be both breathtaking and crushing.

One client explained her experience this way:

> *When I was in my teens, I was awe-inspired by colors and details of my environment. I could not help but burst with excitement and want to express how I perceived the beauty. Realizing this made me look naïve or as if I were seeing the world altered by drugs, I realized it was best to keep my enthusiasm and comments to myself. But that was painful and a reminder that no one understands.*

Many of my clients talk about feeling like they are "too much" for people. Because their intensity tends to overwhelm others, they are told to calm down or quiet down or, as one of my clients put it, to "shallow up." They internalize the message that something is seriously wrong with them. My client Carmen spoke about the shame she carried from years of rejection in her family for her exuberance. She remembered that her talents were criticized or ignored so that she stopped writing poetry and drawing, both activities that she loved. When she read books, which was another passion as well as an escape, she was told by her parents that she was not doing anything worthwhile. She did not feel smart or talented. She felt worthless.

Over time, in therapy, Carmen began to acknowledge her intensity and sensitivity as positive qualities. She remembered her earlier connections to trees and animals and how she talked with them and felt their love. In comparing herself to the ocean, she reflected that she was deep, certainly, but not "too much." But, how can the ocean be too much?

Abundance

In the literature about giftedness, quite a bit has been written about the work of Kazimierz Dabrowski, a Polish psychiatrist who studied gifted youth. He coined the term "overexcitabilities" (OEs) to explain the intensity and sensitivity often seen in gifted children. These OEs can be described as "an abundance of physical, sensual, creative, intellectual, and emotional energy."[10] Placing the rainforest traits within this context is useful because they are not, then, considered dysfunctional. Instead, they are seen as an aspect of temperament that is natural in this population.

I am not going to present details of Dabrowski's theories here; many articles and a few books are available which discuss them.[11] But, I will briefly mention his Theory of Positive Disintegration (TPD) because I have found it quite helpful to RFMs, who tell me they often feel as though they are falling apart or breaking down.

In his TPD, Dabrowski explained that gifted individuals seem to always be reaching for something better, something more worthy in themselves, an evolution of sorts. Along with their "higher levels of empathy, sensitivity, moral responsibility, self-reflection, and autonomy" often resides "intense inner conflict, feelings of inferiority toward their own ideals, feelings of inadequacy, shame and guilt, and existential anxiety and despair."[12]

My client, Keith, tall, thin, and 19, worried, "I have to understand how everything works. Everything." Later, he added, "I have this fantasy that I'm going to be a rocket scientist but I'm so scared of failing. I let everyone down if I'm not Einstein. . . . There's something I need to do for the human race."

But, according to Dabrowski, the rumination is all in the service of growth, increased moral complexity, and higher functioning. Wouldn't it be nice to think of your frequent angst-ridden thinking jags as precursors to breakthroughs, or even necessary for substantial mental-emotional-spiritual expansion? Dabrowski would say that is exactly what they are.

Mary-Elaine Jacobsen, a psychotherapist and writer who works with gifted adults, adds that her clients are often quite self-critical and self-doubting, minimizing their intelligence or even feeling as though they are fooling others and not really as smart as people think they are. It is counterintuitive, but true, that the brightest among us may be the last ones to see it.[13]

Author Amy Tan described her sensitivity this way: "Oftentimes, parents or teachers do not realize how these very things that seem little—a little praise, a little criticism, a little failure—can create such enormous turmoil in a young person's life."[14] Especially if the person has a rainforest mind.

It is often assumed that people who are very smart are also self-confident, perhaps even arrogant, and certainly not bothered by criticism. But the RFM is full of more questions than answers and is more open to possibility and vulnerability. In that state lies greater opportunity to be misunderstood by people who think in more black-and-white terms. I suspect that RFMs are generally more introspective, too, which results in more fault-finding from both self and others and a greater need for solitude and daydreaming.

Beauty and Wonder

Annemarie Roeper, educator, author, and co-founder of the Roeper School for gifted children, described RFM intensity as "a heightened capacity to appreciate beauty and the wonderment in our universe." She said:

[The gifted] see the beauty of human relations, of nature, of literature. They deeply experience the richness of the world around them; hearing beautiful music, seeing a lovely landscape, watching a child grow, observing life, feeling empathy with others. . . . Many gifted people never lose their sense of wonderment. Because there is greater awareness, many things are felt more deeply.[15]

Linda, an adolescent client, described her sensitivities as "being in tune with others' feelings and . . . knowing trees have souls and angels frolic in twilight and wind whispers haikus across the raging Pacific . . . seeing, hearing, and feeling what is invisible to others."

You may ask, doesn't everyone feel this way? And I would answer, yes and no. Certainly, many people are intense, sensitive, and empathetic. But, it is a matter of degree. As an RFM, you just have more of it. Perhaps a lot more. And while beauty and justice might be important to many people, you might find them indispensable.

The empathy Roeper mentions usually begins at an early age. When you were younger, you may have worried about suffering children around the world and felt frustration, guilt, and sadness at your inability to help. You may now have trouble in groups because you deeply feel one person's anger and another's disappointment. It hits you in the stomach or the back of your neck and you are left feeling sick and confused.

Your empathy might also be part of an intuitive capacity that has confused you. Clairvoyance, psychic ability, or tuning into subtle invisible realms could be abilities that you have that you have been afraid to explore.[16] Stephanie Tolan, writer of young adult fiction and frequent speaker on the topic of gifted children, described her journey from logic and science to intuition. In her research and her personal life, she had experiences of the metaphysical or the paranormal. Both in her writing and in encounters with nature, she felt a deep connection with something larger than herself and a knowing beyond her own cognition.[17]

Andrew, an athletic client of mine, described his empathy and sensitivity in nature this way:

Growing up in a very rural and wooded area, I have always felt a close connection with nature but a heightened awareness of trees specifically. I have been brought to tears numerous times when I've seen trees cut down or even if they have been overly trimmed. It's similar to the feeling of loss I have experienced with the death of loved ones.

Intensity, sensitivity, and empathy, then, are not often included in the stereotypical description of a highly intelligent individual. Yet, evidence in the literature and in my own experience suggests otherwise. In the following two client profiles, I have emphasized these particular traits. At the same time, you will see that these individuals possess all of the characteristics highlighted in this book.

Billy: What's Wrong with Me?

Billy, 16, had been experiencing severe anxiety, missing several days of school. His mother described him as "hard on himself," a "perfectionist," and "very sensitive." He felt judged, misunderstood, and bullied by peers. Never identified in school as gifted, Billy assumed there was something seriously wrong with him. He knew he was different, but he did not know why.

Billy's very active mind spent lots of time worrying. He was aware that "small stuff" would snowball into enormous anxiety, but he did not know how to control it.

I met with Billy and his parents in our first session. His parents were supportive, empathetic professionals who understood sensitivity in general, but never put it in the context of giftedness. They were open to the information I presented and the reading I suggested.

Tall and slim with deeply kind brown eyes and a sweet smile, Billy always wore the same dark grey hooded sweatshirt and black slacks. At every session, even during the summer heat wave, he kept the hood up, covering long brown hair that was swept across his forehead.

I could see that Billy's levels of empathy and sensitivity were extraordinary as he thoughtfully responded to my statements and talked about people, animals, and nature with care and respect. I could tell by the concerned look on his face that he was also very tuned to my reactions and attentive to my well-being. He said, "I pick up things others don't. If a person is having a bad day, it rubs off on me," "I have to carry other people's weight. I don't want someone to feel bad," and, "I want to help my friends, it's who I am. . . . It's like having a bigger net. But the net gets full and it sinks the ship."

I saw that Billy readily sensed the emotions of his fellow adolescents, and I suggested to Billy that a school environment would be difficult if for no other reason than he would feel bombarded by the sounds, smells, florescent lights, and intensity in the building.

He described his experiences with test-taking and writing. With tests, Billy would know the material but become anxious if there was a time limit. Sometimes, he would over-think the questions and either choose the wrong answer because of the divergent thinking he would use to analyze the situation or never finish the test because he had taken too much time to respond. On multiple choice tests, he could come up with reasons why each answer could be correct. His poor grades did not reflect his intelligence and he began to think he was stupid. Some of his teachers assumed he was either lazy or not capable; his parents were confused.

With writing, Billy was extremely thoughtful and precise. Again, time pressures and his own desire for clarity created so much tension that Billy often could not complete assignments. He said that he did not think he had adequate writing ability, although he admitted that he had scored 110 percent on an essay that he did hand in for a teacher who understood him and had flexible deadlines.

Eventually, Billy started to feel relief as he accepted that being easily overwhelmed and anxious was at least partly due to his sensitivities and empathy. We agreed that anxiety is more complicated when you can think of many reasons to be distressed and when you find multiple variables within each of the reasons.

Billy spoke about his deep love of music and his desire to become a musician and make a difference for others. He described the hours he spent practicing and figuring out innovative ways to play his guitar. His passion was palpable as he looked for the words to describe how his soul needed music. This desire, combined with his high standards, led to severe frustration and discouragement when he felt that he was not living up to his own expectations. He explained, "I have very high standards that advance my playing and I get new ideas. But I beat myself up when it doesn't happen right. My emotion of not being good enough overshadows my reason."

Protection from the Harsh World

During one session, Billy said he was feeling overwhelmed with anxiety again, and that so many little things could start the cycle that it was hard to stay calm. He felt out-of-control and as though his emotions and memories were flooding his awareness. "I worry about the past, the present, my retirement. I don't believe in myself. It's a wonder I'm not even more of a mess." He questioned whether he could trust this new "template" of having a rainforest mind. He wanted to hold onto the worry so as not to be disappointed once again, or hurt, particularly by people who continued to misunderstand him.

I explained to Billy how his limbic system was triggered when he was anxious and how talking and moving could bring him back into his more rational mind. I also introduced a couple of techniques he could use at home and at school. Along with deep breathing, I explained how he could focus on the tension in his body, rather than on his emotions. He could just notice it and feel it. Allowing the sensations to simply "be" might actually permit them to shift.

Billy described the tightness in his back and chest, but upon breathing into it and allowing it, he started to feel "lighter." At first, he was skeptical whenever I introduced a new technique, though he seemed to incorporate it later. Being analytical like Billy, RFMs can be skeptical when presented with a new idea.

As time went on, Billy's self-understanding and confidence increased. He was considering transferring to a small charter school that seemed to be a good match for his learning style and sensitivities. The structure of the school was based around discussion and student-initiated projects. Classrooms had comfortable sofas and beanbag chairs. Energetic teachers were interested in connecting deeply with their students.

When Billy enrolled, he found teachers who appreciated his intensity, sensitivity, and curiosity, in a relaxed flexible atmosphere. On a couple of occasions, though, Billy was again overwhelmed and had to leave school early. One time, the class was talking about genocide. Another, a boy had killed an insect. Both experiences hurt Billy deeply and he could not calm himself. Surprisingly, his teachers and classmates were sympathetic. He was not bullied, teased, or told to "get over it."

Billy told me that he did not reveal his strong feelings to his parents when he was younger as a way to protect them. From a very young age, he also felt he had to figure things out on his own. He recalled thinking at age six, "I should know the answer to this. I should do it right the first time." He recalled insisting on learning cursive writing in second grade and wanting to learn the Chinese language in third.

When I asked if he thought he might be carrying a large build-up of unexpressed emotion, he described his emotions as "a dormant volcano erupting," which he now felt safe enough to release.

Know Everything Before I Learn It

Billy described a new interest in guitar electronics, and how he was driven to know everything about it down to the "atomic level," while simultaneously studying "music theory and harmonic analysis." When I reminded him that this was typical RFM behavior, he added that he remembered even in first grade how his RFM traits were at play. "I've always wanted to know everything before I learned it," he said.

Billy was making progress. He had decided to learn to play the ukulele and the violin, instruments that were new to him, and he continued to play drums at school in front of his peers. In trying new instruments, he risked not being the best and he experimented with playing for fun, which challenged the perfectionist in him.

As our work continued, Billy suffered recurrences of serious anxiety. After one particularly intense period, we discussed self-soothing strategies again. The one that worked the best was finding ways to distract himself with different activities such as researching topics of interest online, rebuilding his bike, or learning computer coding. He also grew more comfortable with sharing his fears with his mother and letting her comfort him. He went on drives with his father, which helped deepen their connection.

Even though music was the center of his universe, Billy enjoyed multiple interests. Exploring and expanding these interests was pleasurable and therapeutic. He enjoyed archery, basketball, electronics, blacksmithing, and woodworking. He also liked auto mechanics, theoretical physics, pencil-sketching, and computer code. He was rebuilding an old guitar and carving a wooden flute. I encouraged Billy to experiment with doing these activities for pleasure, and reducing the self-imposed pressure to be thorough and exacting.

Billy also grappled with his great desire to be of service to all living beings and with his tendency to become overwhelmed by all the suffering he saw and felt. He learned that he did not need to absorb someone else's pain to help them and that exhausting himself in the process would not serve anyone in the long run. He expressed concern about several of his peers in school, wondering how to help them. First, I reminded him that self-care was not selfish. Then, I suggested that compassion and healthy boundaries were compatible. He realized that he needed to set limits to his involvement in his friends' problems so that he would have the energy to be more effective in the long term.

Over time, Billy reported more and more progress. He understood his rainforest mind and appreciated his sensitivities, empathy, intensity, and divergent thinking. He also had greater control over his anxiety.

He gradually cut back on his counseling visits. At one of our last sessions, he strode into my office in a black leather jacket and an air of confidence. He told me that he'd recently given a speech at his high school graduation, a feat that would have been impossible one year earlier. "I still feel self-conscious but it's different. . . . The most important thing that's changed is I don't feel so closed," he said. "If something doesn't work, I don't feel it's doomsday anymore. I can make mistakes and feel anxious, but not let it get the best of me. I've reached this really great balance."

Billy no longer felt that something was wrong with him. His sensitive, open heart was ready to sing.

Janice: Magical Kingdoms

Janice, 23, a petite young woman with big brown eyes and dramatic short platinum hair, came to counseling because she was depressed and experiencing fears that kept her from attending college classes. She was afraid she would have to drop out if she could not get her anxiety under control. She struggled with extreme anxiety which hindered her ability to fulfill her goals, as well as create lasting relationships with friends and family. She mentioned an estranged relationship with her divorced parents and a suicide attempt in high school.

In a journal entry Janice shared with me, she wrote, "I'm just so afraid all the time. I'm tired of carrying all this around. Of choking on fear, in my throat and my heart. It's got a stranglehold on my life and I cannot move forward."

Janice had frequent nightmares and trouble sleeping and she often skipped meals. Even though she was a French major at the time and got good grades on papers when she did attend classes, Janice had no confidence in her abilities and felt hopeless about her capacity to be successful, either in school or in life.

Janice told me that she thought the rainforest mind analogy was intriguing, but like many people, she did not see herself as gifted. When I explained the traits of the RFM, she was surprised at how much she fit the profile. Though she had never been identified as gifted in school, she explained that she was frequently called too sensitive, too serious, and a show-off because she was highly emotional and intense about living life to the fullest. Janice talked about her sensitivities to the hum of ceiling fans, foods that have the right flavor but the wrong texture (or the right texture and the wrong flavor), transcendent music, other people's feelings, the color of someone's eyes, and the "haunting plum color of a dying sunset." I suspected that some of her anxiety was due to her sensitivities and ability to sense other people's feelings.

Family Dynamics

In examining her family of origin, Janice described what I determined was likely an alcoholic, abusive, narcissistic mother and a neglectful father. She had been both emotionally and physically abused. To cope as a child, Janice used her sensitivity to imagine her own worlds and magical kingdoms. She spent lots of time in her favorite willow tree.

I explained her symptoms using the diagnosis post-traumatic stress disorder (PTSD). In typical RFM style, she researched everything she could about the topic, including a book she found called *The PTSD Sourcebook*. I recommended *The Anxiety and Phobia Workbook*, by Edmund Bourne and *Procrastination*, by Jane Burka and Lenora Yuen. She read them eagerly.

Even though Janice experienced serious anxiety and depression with suicidal thoughts due to her early trauma, she was insightful and articulate during sessions. Her perky energy might have masked her deep despair if I had not seen this pattern many times before. In part, her cheerfulness was a coping strategy, but it was also a reflection of her idealism and resilience, typical RFM characteristics.

I suspect that some counselors are confused by these clients' apparent vitality. They may not realize the depth of the individual's pain because he or she looks fine and, in many cases, is highly functional. I have seen many clients with these paradoxical feelings and behaviors. It seems that RFMs can deeply appreciate the beauty of an ancient redwood or the wonder of the ocean even while experiencing the fear of abandonment and intense self-hatred.

In the beginning of our time together, Janice and I worked on strategies to help her feel less anxious so that she could attend her classes. We also sought out the reasons for her anxiety and her depression. Janice felt the need to understand the source of her problems so that she could truly find self-acceptance.

I work from a psychodynamic model with most of my clients, since a thorough answering of the "why" questions and the desire for a thorough processing is often required for resolution of the problem. The RFM does not settle for shallow or simplistic answers. Consequently, Janice spent some time telling me what she remembered about her early years. During this time, we were not only seeking an understanding of how she became so fearful, but also forming a bond that could begin to repair some of her early abandonment experiences. As is true of most clients, Janice carried a lot of self-blame. She told me that she felt "defective" and "weak and stupid." She felt responsible for taking care of her parents but, at the same time, was furious with them.

In another journal entry, she wrote:

> I feel like the world just wants me to forgive them, to just let it go and act like, even though they're responsible, that I shouldn't make them acknowledge it. Because they gave birth to me, or they raised me. [Expletive.] Honestly. I think they should HAVE to acknowledge it because they ARE my parents, not get out of it. Being a parent is a [expletive] responsibility and it's hard. But I had no one to protect me and they let me down. . . . This isn't my fault and yet I'm the one dying inside.

In identifying the level of abuse Janice experienced, my intention was not to heap blame on the parents, but to hold them fully accountable for their choices and their serious mistakes. I wanted to help Janice understand that she was not responsible for the chaos and abuse in her family. Confronting her parents directly was not the goal; in fact, that can often be retraumatizing. Instead, our goal was to understand the effects of the abuse, process Janice's feelings in our safe therapy setting, and come to a place of peace.

It became clear that Janice needed extra support to get to classes, complete assignments, and consistently keep her therapy appointments. There were many days when she could not leave her home. We talked about the possible use of antidepressants. I do not usually recommend medication unless a client cannot function well enough to accomplish basic tasks or to get the benefits of psychotherapy, which was the case with Janice. While she was reluctant to use medication, she met with her doctor and decided to try a low dose. Within a few weeks, Janice gained enough energy and motivation to continue school and come to our sessions.

The Self as Bedrock

Using Internal Family Systems theory, a therapy model developed by psychologist Richard Schwartz (*Internal Family Systems Therapy*, 1997), Janice identified several subpersonalities dwelling within her, including a wounded child, a critic, a hopeless part, and introjects (internalized parental voices). She also identified a Self (what Schwartz sees as each person's true essence) that she could feel in her body, which she called her "bedrock." Janice located the bedrock in her belly. Using this process, Janice learned to talk with these various parts of herself in her journal and negotiate with them to create a gradual growing sense of self-worth.

One of the parts Janice worked with was her perfectionism. She procrastinated on school assignments and avoided writing projects. Writing, in particular, was so important to her that she became paralyzed when facing the blank page. In our sessions, we talked about the source of perfectionism in RFMs and looked at how the pressure to be smart played out in Janice's life. She wrote:

> *I lie about the depth of my knowledge because I cannot look stupid ever. I don't know how much of that is my childhood appearing inside my procrastination, but I guess it really doesn't matter. I can't just say, "No, I've never seen that movie." I love random facts about various topics, but I have lied about knowing things. I make them up so that I can stay in my safe little bubble.*

The pressure can be that great.

Body Awareness and the Bad Robot Dance

In one session, Janice talked about a project designing a website that she had agreed, weeks ago, to complete for her father. She had yet to start it. Using a body-centered approach, similar to psychotherapist Peter Levine's somatic experiencing (*Waking the Tiger: Healing Trauma*, 1997), we examined what was keeping Janice from moving forward. We began with her tuning in to how her body felt as she thought about starting this project. She was aware of a "choking" in her throat, tension in her arms, and a "sick ball of guilt" in her abdomen where she felt she was "mourning." We just noticed the movement of the sensations, without judgment.

Then Janice said she felt that she had to "sit still and not fidget because fidgeting would be disrespectful." I suggested she try moving and notice what happened. She reported feeling angry and then sad. Continuing to notice her body's sensations, Janice started to move more and said she felt like doing her "bad robot dance." She explained, "I do this dance when I win a video game. It's my victory dance." Even though she said she was embarrassed, she showed me the dance. She did some subtle hip-hop moves with her upper body that relaxed her tension and got her laughing. I suggested that moving/dancing could be quite therapeutic and might help to break Janice's pattern of anxiety. She agreed to try it on her own.

I then had her make a list of the steps she needed to take to start the website project. This list was easy to generate. As it got longer, Janice noticed her anxiety returning, so I suggested she put the long list away and focus on the next three steps that she felt were achievable. When she started to feel tension rising, she executed some small motions of her robot dance with her arms and felt herself laugh and relax again. She was able to imagine starting the work on the website later that day.

Janice spent many sessions expressing her frustrations and sadness about the abuse she suffered in her childhood and her present strained relationships with her parents. Grieving childhood losses takes time, particularly when you are a highly sensitive, intense, and empathetic individual. It is a delicate process because of the intricate layers of emotion and experience. But after working in counseling for about two years, Janice graduated from college and planned to apply to grad school. She had a newly acquired confidence in her future. She had completed the website for her father, which not only felt like a solid accomplishment but also led her to explore the computer science field. She started a blog where she began to put her stories out in the world.

In an assessment of her progress, Janice said that she could now understand and accept her parents' limitations and keep herself safe from her still-alcoholic mother. She was able to list sensitivity, intensity, and empathy as positive traits and acknowledge her courage. She could access her true Self through her belly, and said that her bedrock told her, "We can make things happen." And she did.

Strategies

❧ Protect yourself when you feel assaulted by noise, smells, emotions, thoughts, chemicals, bad architecture, etc. Leave places early, step away from someone, wear a hooded sweatshirt, visualize protection around you, get grounded in your body, or breathe slowly and deeply. Other possibilities include imagining a "power animal" to protect you, shrieking in your car, singing, getting physical, using ear plugs and sunglasses, and getting out into nature. For additional support and ideas, read *The Highly Sensitive Person*, by Elaine Aron.

❧ Keep a journal where you can write, draw, collage, and/or paint. It is important to have expressive outlets that allow you to be as "much" as you are.

❧ You may find it hard to fall asleep and/or stay asleep if your thoughts are racing. Use stress reduction techniques and get physical exercise during the day. Before going to bed, make a list of what is on your mind and tell yourself you can pick it back up in the morning. Listen to calming music. Use ear plugs and an eye mask. Try different combinations of melatonin and/or herbal remedies until you find the right mix. If you do not want to sleep because you are afraid of missing out on something fascinating, remember that your dreams can be just as exciting as your waking life. Try the 4-7-8 technique: Breathe in through your nose for 4, hold for 7, and breathe out through your mouth for 8. Check online for ideas: New technologies are appearing every day to help with sleep and relaxation.

❧ Check to see if you have any food allergies or food sensitivities. A good nutritionist can help with this. Your body is likely as sensitive as your heart and mind.

- If you have lived for years thinking something was wrong with you because of your sensitivities and intensities, it may take time for a new, positive identity to sink in and take hold. Give yourself a chance to process any feelings you may have about the years of misperceptions of yourself. Do not expect the switch to happen quickly. A new template does not just appear. You will be clearing out the old, grieving, saying good-bye, and slipping back and forth into old patterns and beliefs many times along the way.

- Your fabulous, creative mind will take you on all sorts of ruminating and catastrophizing adventures. Try to recognize when this is happening and breathe, exercise, get out into nature, or do something that requires intense focus such as tai chi, ballet, Pilates, or rock climbing. Use your analytical mind or a good friend or therapist to provide a reality check.

- Set healthy boundaries with your children, parents, partner, neighbors, colleagues, pets, and friends—anyone who has needs who might be asking (directly or indirectly) for help. Just because you are really good at supporting and guiding others does not mean you ought to do it all the time. Say "no" when you need time and space for yourself. Others will benefit when you model healthy boundary-setting and you'll be more ready to help when it really counts.

- Find activities that allow you to be intense. Try debate, chess, running marathons, or contra dancing.

- If you have children like you, remember that they will be quite emotional and intense and may say things like "I hate you" or "You're the worst parent ever" in the heat of the moment and not really mean it. You may wonder how such a smart kid can be so dumb sometimes, but remember that the nature of the RFM is to have big feelings. Try not to take it personally. In response, use techniques suggested in *Raising Your Spirited Child*, such as active listening, natural consequences, good boundaries, and avoidance of power struggles.

🐚 The book *Healing Through the Dark Emotions*, by Miriam Greenspan, is an excellent resource if you want to do some deep psychological work.

🐚 If you notice yourself feeling frequently overwhelmed or enraged by your child, he or she may be triggering some pain from your past. Journal about your feelings and see if the situation feels familiar; it may be that you are unconsciously re-enacting an experience from your past. This is a fairly common occurrence; however, it is generally not easy to analyze these underground emotions without the help of a therapist. So, if you are frequently over-reacting to your child's big feelings, consider psychotherapy.

🐚 Learn some self-soothing techniques to calm your emotions and your nervous system. Make a list of things that relax you, such as taking a warm bath or listening to classical music. Look into massage, herbal remedies, rescue remedy, flower essences, essential oils, amino acids such as L-theanine, or CDs from healthjourneys.com. Also, try exercise, mindfulness, prayer, yoga, painting, therapeutic touch, energy work, acupuncture, or tai chi. Avoid pot and alcohol. Read *The Mood Cure*, by Julia Ross, if you are dealing with fatigue, depression, or anxiety.

🐚 Read *The HeartMath Solution* for a set of tools that incorporate the neurons in your heart to help build a sense of relaxation, calm, and an "access route" to your intuition.

🐚 If you find yourself frequently drawn to people who are particularly needy, either in friendships or intimate relationships, remember that you can be compassionate without exhausting yourself. The more you take care of yourself, the better able you will be to contribute. There are ways to give without depleting your own energy. You will be more effective with more people if you select situations that best fit your particular skills, interests, and desires and if you let go of the need to save everyone. It is all right to be careful with your energy and time; in fact, it is necessary, if you want to live your fullest life.

ॐ Read Donna Eden's book, *Energy Medicine: Balancing Your Body's Energies for Optimal Health, Joy and Vitality,* for some more unusual ways to soothe your nervous system.

ॐ If you are female and near menopause or post-menopausal, find a practitioner who has studied women's hormones to get good information and support in navigating this tricky terrain. Ellen Dolgen has a good website with information: www.shmirshky.com

ॐ If you are having intuitive insights or psychic experiences that are worrying you, read Judith Orloff, Caroline Myss, and others on developing intuition. Find resources at soundstrue.com and noetic.org. Look for a mentor. Consider exploring "non-ordinary reality" or the invisible world by studying shamanism and learning shamanic journeying. Read Sandra Ingerman's books. It could be that intuition is a tool that you can use to access new ideas and your authentic Self. You may feel crazy. You are not.

Chapter Two

If You're So Smart,
Why Aren't You Saving the World

Compassion hurts. When you feel connected to everything, you also feel responsible for everything. And you cannot turn away. Your destiny is bound with the destinies of others. You must either learn to carry the Universe or be crushed by it. You must grow strong enough to love the world, yet empty enough to sit down at the same table with its worst horrors.

To seek enlightenment is to seek annihilation, rebirth, and the taking up of burdens. You must become prepared to touch and be touched by every thing in heaven and hell.

~Andrew Boyd[18]

Connected to Everything

In my counseling practice, RFMs not only are troubled by their own personal psychological issues and traumas, but also deeply concerned about the state of the world and the suffering of others, including plants, animals, and ecosystems.[19] They can have an early awareness of environmental and social justice issues and an intense desire to take action. In *The Gifted Adult*, Mary-Elaine Jacobsen observes:

*Perceptivity is often associated with issues of unfairness, a topic
that tends to bring on outrage in many gifted individuals. Intense
reactions to inequity and cruelty are normal. . . . Oftentimes the
client reveals a feeling of being tugged toward an unclear legacy or
to advocate for change, as though it were a call to duty.*[20]

Charles Eisenstein, political activist and author of *Sacred
Economics*, experiences it this way: "I have oft encountered a deep
anguish and helplessness borne out of the ubiquity of the world-
devouring machine and of the near-impossibility of avoiding
participation in it."[21]

Existential depression can result when you feel powerless and
overwhelmed by sociopolitical issues and events and when you do not
know how you can contribute adequately. At an early age you may have
asked the big questions, like "Why am I here?" or "What gives life
meaning?" or even "Why are humans so cruel?" Now, you may feel
great frustration and guilt as you go about your own busy life and you
are not finding the cure for Alzheimer's disease or singlehandedly
ending global warming. And if you received early messages about how
"smart" you are, you may put excessive pressure on yourself to achieve
at the highest levels. You experience ongoing frustration with your
inability to measure up.[22]

You may feel guilt because you:
- Were told that you have great potential but feel you are not using it
- Feel responsible for all of the suffering on the planet
- Live a privileged life
- Want to feed the hungry person with the sign on the corner but do not
- Have not won a Nobel prize

And when you talk with people about this guilt and existential
depression, you hear, "You're too idealistic. Get real," or "You worry
too much." Or, worse yet, you may be asked, "If you are so smart, why

aren't you doing something important?" Needless to say, these responses are not helpful.

Psychologist Patricia Gatto-Walden's research revealed that profoundly gifted students in middle school and high school were determined to build lives of meaning, making significant contributions to society. A group of gifted women whom she studied expressed similar needs, along with guilt and frustration when family responsibilities or the mundane world called for their attention.[23]

One of my teen clients asked, "How do I understand the world? What's the point of life?" When I responded with a question about her personal search for purpose, I heard the impatience in her voice when she said, "It's not just about me." Clearly, she had a larger question in mind—one that I was unprepared to answer. Luckily, RFM clients are not looking to me for answers. Many times, we just dive into the mystery together and swim around in the questions.

Hope and Idealism

Interestingly, existential depression can be coupled with idealism.[24] Even as they are aware of the great suffering on the planet, many RFMs continue to hold a sense of hope, gratitude, and appreciation for the beauty and preciousness of life. They are often accused of naiveté and, when they are younger, immaturity. I recall teenage clients of mine refusing to be cynical or hang out at the mall (or on social media) with the "cool" kids, not due to some missing maturity, but due to a maturity beyond their years.

RFMs often have an unusual sense that human potential is much greater than we imagine. Eisenstein describes it as a "heart-knowledge" of our "native radiance."[25] A "very sensitive, intellectual and dreamy child," Eisenstein defends his idealism in his article, "Naiveté, and the Light in their Eyes." He says that some of his readers assume that he cannot really know "the magnitude of the present [environmental] crisis" and still be optimistic. But he may, in fact, be a visionary tuned in to something that the cynics cannot see, and so he holds a positive view of future possibilities.[26]

Mary, a young single mother, was a good example of someone with a strong sense of justice. Because of her severe depression, we spoke about the possibility of taking anti-depressants for a short period of time. She had grown up with an alcoholic mother and a meth-addicted father, and was struggling financially. Her depression was not just existential, although she was clearly disturbed about the state of the world. Even though she was overwhelmed by grad school requirements and raising her young son on her own, she had strong convictions about how she needed to contribute to making the world a better place.

Mary declined the medication, not based on concerns about side effects, but out of a desire to not support the pharmaceutical companies which, she believed, were part of a corporate structure only interested in acquiring wealth. This led to a discussion of why she would not shop at Walmart for her son's school clothes (because the corporation refused to pay employees a living wage). Clearly her sense of justice had trumped her personal welfare. I was not surprised.

The RFMs I have known have pretty consistently felt responsible for creating a better world. Bill Plotkin, psychotherapist and author of *Soulcraft* and other books about the healing power of the natural world, describes his perspective this way:

> *The gift you carry for others is not an attempt to save the world but to fully belong to it. It's not possible to save the world by trying to save it. You need to find what is genuinely yours to offer the world before you can make it a better place. Discovering your unique gift to bring to your community is your greatest opportunity and challenge. The offering of that gift—your true self—is the most you can do to love and serve the world. And it is all the world needs.*[27]

Gwen: Belonging to the World

Gwen, 52, came to counseling because she had plunged into depression after completing her PhD. She said she wanted to find the best way to make an impact on society, but was unsure how to proceed. Her research, which combined art, the social sciences, and world history all through the feminist perspective, made her acutely aware of the enormous suffering of women around the world.

She grappled with how to live with a consciousness of the extent of the harm and the pervasiveness of "white privilege." Additionally, she wondered what the right thing to do was. What would have the greatest positive impact? How could she be happy when so many others were in pain? How could she respond to people who told her to "lighten up" or "don't make waves." In counseling, she had a safe place to feel her despair, tap into her intuition, and find her creative, authentic path.

Gwen learned that many RFMs experience existential depression—the condition she was struggling with when she began seeing me. She felt reassured learning that RFMs naturally possess high levels of morality and justice concerns.

Gwen came to a subsequent session in great distress. She had just seen the documentary *Gasland*,[28] which described fracking, the practice in which natural gas is extracted from shale rock deep underground. She expressed her serious concerns for the many people, creatures, and plants living in surrounding communities that, according to the documentary, were being poisoned by fracking.

Gwen could not just ignore this information. She was feeling grief for the individuals already made ill and for the future of our country's land, water, and air. We talked about the activist organization that evolved from the documentary and other groups such as 350.org and Joanna Macy's environmental work. Gwen's desire to positively change the way humans function was in high gear. Fracking was just one of numerous activities that disturbed her.

Gwen deeply felt the suffering of humans, animals, and plants. At times she felt nearly paralyzed by despair. It can be hard to be that sensitive and aware. But this considerable sensitivity and high awareness seem to be the reality of the RFM. As Andrew Boyd observed at the beginning of this chapter, "When you feel connected to everything, you feel responsible for everything." And it hurts.

Quiet Down, Slow Down

Gwen mentioned that as a child, she talked to redwood trees. She felt they were sacred beings. She also had felt that they, like other trees or animals, would speak to her sometimes. Like Janice (profiled in Chapter One), others typically found her "too sensitive" and "too much" and advised her not to "take everything so seriously." For most of her life, she had not been identified as gifted. Through counseling, she was trying to reconnect to her authenticity as a way to find her true work in the world and to ease the loneliness she had felt all her life.

Gwen had a mixed response to her rainforest-minded traits. On the one hand, she was relieved. At the same time, she felt discouraged that she might continue to feel deeply lonely if she could not find others whom she could truly relate to and collaborate with.

In later counseling sessions, it became apparent that growing up Gwen had been her family's scapegoat. Initially, she said her childhood had been fine, but when she described her parents in more detail, it became clear that from an early age they had depended on her for emotional support. Gwen was able to see that she had experienced much shame in her family, around both her physical appearance and her multiple talents. Her family seemed to think that she was not pretty enough and not feminine enough. She had loved drawing, painting, and writing poetry, but was greeted with criticism instead of encouragement. She internalized the parental messages that she was "not enough" in some ways, while "too much" in others. As a result, she had stopped creating visual art and poetry, cut off her spiritual connection to nature, and did not recognize the depth of her intellect.

I have seen many other cases where young gifted children become the support for the parents if the family is either dysfunctional or abusive. Often, the RFM is capable of handling more than other children her age. This premature burden of parental support can set the child up later to feel overly responsible for others. She then feels frightened and like a failure if she does not always know the answers. Even in the absence of abuse in a family, the RFM whose parents depended on her too much can put pressure on herself to always excel and will feel crushed if she does not measure up.

Inconsequential Joy

In spite of her enormous personal and collective grief, Gwen also felt gratitude:

> *I am so utterly grateful for where I live, what (and who) I see out my windows because the beauty, the daily astonishing wonder of all these lovely beings, all this amazing diverse gorgeous life does help fill the hollows in my soul that grief and despair carve out. Thank goodness for all the beauty, wonder, and daily quiet radiance! The carving seems pretty relentless at times.*

Despite the hollows, Gwen told me that small, seemingly "inconsequential" moments could bring her great joy. Just that week, she was overwhelmed by how the colors of the walls in her bedroom changed when the sky was clear and the late afternoon light reflected off the green birch leaves into the space. She felt she was "basking in beauty." Before knowing about her RFM, she might have hidden this experience in embarrassment. Now, she could celebrate the awareness that brought her such an intense experience, even if others might misinterpret her passion.

At our next session, Gwen reported that she felt ready to complete this round of counseling. She had connected with an agent to look at her book proposal and was excitedly writing chapter titles. She had signed up for a writer's conference to make more contacts with agents and planned to attend a professional conference where several prominent researchers were speaking. Gwen also joined a Toastmasters group in anticipation of her future role presenting to the public.

Some months later, I heard from Gwen and we had another set of sessions. It is not unusual for RFMs to examine their inner worlds in an ongoing way throughout their lives. This time, she was working on understanding the shame she felt in her childhood family and how it had affected her marriages, her health, and her self-esteem. During this period, Gwen expressed a deeper layer of personal grief. She had come to wonder if she would ever truly receive love for her authentic self. She cried as the pain washed over her. She had always been a caretaker of others and wondered whether she could allow herself some "healthy selfishness." She left that session with a list of suggestions and reminders to build a self-care practice.

At our next meeting, Gwen brought in a collage that she had made. Melding beautiful blues, purples, and greens, images of oceans and trees, she had intuitively expressed her authenticity. She recognized herself as a weaver, taking many strands from many disciplines and creating an extraordinary tapestry.

In time, Gwen learned to hold herself in the same esteem that she held others. She realized that her capacity for joy dove as deep as her grief. She came to know that her idealism and intelligence could wield the kind of impact that she dreamed of.

Gwen understood her rainforest mind. She explained:

Perhaps we gifted folk are being hollowed out a bit—emotionally, consciously, psychically—so that it is easier for the currents of universal love and delight to lift us up, to help us be aloft and nimble, just as the hollow bones and feathers enable birds the means to fly.

Gwen brought her rainforest intelligence into the world—and she flew.

Beth: Creating a Life that Matters

Beth's mom, Virginia, contacted me because her 16-year-old daughter wanted to see a counselor. Virginia told me that Beth was "underachieving and generally apathetic about life" and that she had experienced some early trauma with a dad who had been addicted to drugs and physically abusive. In the initial phone call, Virginia told me that Beth had excelled in school through eighth grade—that she had been popular, athletic, and high-achieving—but that now she was sleeping a lot and lonely. "It's a dramatic change," Virginia explained.

At our first session, Beth, a muscular, tall, articulate girl with short cropped auburn hair, identified her concerns and what she wanted to address in counseling. She said that she was not motivated in school and that she had few friends. She said, "I feel like there is no point in life sometimes. I overanalyze a lot, and have anxiety. I often feel sad and don't have many people I can relate to."

Beth's one friend, Maddie, spent most of her time with her boyfriend *du jour* and could not be relied upon for support. When the girls did get together, Beth spent a lot of the time counseling Maddie. Beth found most of her classes uninspiring, although she enjoyed English and "loved" her teacher. She described a class assignment to read the novel *1984* and how she was affected by it and "overanalyzed" the themes, while her peers pronounced the book "stupid."

She said:

> *I wrote a seven-page paper detailing every corrupt thing our country was doing to us and what other countries were also doing and I obsessed over it for months and months after that. Every time I heard about another bill passing about trying to censor the internet, continuing to let Monsanto genetically modify our food, or seeing things like police brutality during the Occupy Wall Street protests, I would connect it back to 1984. All the other kids in the class just thought it was another fantasy story. Just another book you have to read in high school for no apparent reason. I realized the book was meant to help people question the world around them . . . around this time was when I also started feeling really disconnected from my peers at school.*

This incident was typical of her schooling experiences. She longed for a friend who had a similarly questioning mind.

Beth spent a lot of time worrying about the size of the universe, "a world without money, how corrupt everything is between the rich and the poor," the purpose of life in general and hers in particular. On the one hand, she felt life might be pointless; on the other hand, she wondered whether she would be wasting her life if she did not do something important. She wrote:

I am extremely scared of not doing enough with my life and regretting it later, like not trying hard enough in college or not going at all. I'm almost always stuck in this constant paradox of being aware that I am lazy and unmotivated and disliking it and being scared that I'm going to ruin my life and waste it away . . . the feeling is terrifying.

She told me that when she was nine she wanted to be President, but that now she questioned the importance of grades and wished she was "just average" and "could live a simple life." She felt guilty for being depressed and odd for watching documentaries and reading Deepak Chopra.

Beth and I talked about the rainforest mind and how her depression and anxiety were at least partly connected to her sensitivities, empathy, desire to change the world and her active, analytical brain. I served as a listener who could validate the complexity of her worries rather than offer simple, surface solutions. Since her anxiety increased at night, we problem-solved about how she might sleep better with herbal remedies, positive self-talk, and planning ahead to get her schoolwork completed. I gave Beth a list of websites so that she could see what people were accomplishing to address global suffering and the serious environmental issues that she worried about.

We also examined her concerns about friendships. She said that she would like to have a boyfriend, but that she did not find any boys who wanted to talk about politics or "the enormity of the universe."

She knew a few boys as friends, but her experience was that they would be unavailable once they found girlfriends. Both boys and girls her age, she said, were "too interested in superficial things."

We talked about community activities that might serve a dual purpose of connecting with activist organizations and meeting people she could relate to. I suggested she talk with her English teacher about writing groups or other intellectual-social opportunities, and that she look into the local university's ballroom dance club and Argentine tango community. Dance classes could be an easier way to meet new people and also to explore a new way to be athletic. I suggested that Beth check out a local agency that served young women, which offered classes in the arts, body image, biking, trauma recovery, and other topics that might interest her.

Beth wondered about whether college would be worth the money and, if so, how she could afford to go and what she would study. She borrowed the book *Colleges that Change Lives*, by Loren Pope, so that she might start research about a higher education plan that would meet her needs.

Beth's mother, Virginia, also had a rainforest mind and as a teacher had taken classes on giftedness from a local university. Beth was able to tell her about the circumstances underneath her existential depression and anxiety without fear of being misunderstood. Together, they made a plan for the next school year that included taking some classes online and graduating early.

A few weeks later, I received a note from Virginia saying that Beth was ready to stop counseling. Beth's apathy had lifted and her motivation had returned. She had taken a psychology class that sparked an interest in counseling as a possible career path. I hoped that Beth would make the contacts I had suggested. I was confident she would find others wanting to create a better world and that she would take the action she needed to feel that her life mattered. Perhaps, she would even decide to run for President.

Strategies

❧ If you are feeling despair about the state of the world, let yourself feel it. Joanna Macy, the eco-philosopher and scholar, talks about how people going deeply into their despair can actually stumble upon creativity, intuition, and insight down there in the depths. Grieving for the world can open new capacities and solutions that can motivate you into creative action. Find out more about Joanna Macy's positive view of the future at joannamacy.net.

❧ Try the Buddhist tonglen meditation practice of breathing in the suffering of others and breathing out love, as described in Pema Chodron's book and at pemachodronfoundation.org. Since you will likely feel the suffering of others anyway, try breathing into it rather than tensing against it or trying to avoid it. But do not stop there. Feel your openness and your expansiveness and breathe out love to yourself and all others. Imagine that you are tapping into a Love that is always with you and that flows freely through you. (Some RFMs find this technique overwhelming and unhelpful. As with all of these ideas, choose the ones that work for you.)

❧ Read Charles Eisenstein's *The More Beautiful World Our Hearts Know is Possible.*

❧ Find out about organizations within your faith community or online that are making a difference locally or globally. Service clubs, such as Rotary, can be ways to contribute. International organizations, such as avaaz.org and freethechildren.org, focus on worldwide humanitarian concerns.

❧ Practice letting go of guilt. Sit in a comfortable position for meditation. Get an image of your guilt. Is it a sticky piece of gum on the bottom of your shoe? Hands around your throat? Picture your guilt and then imagine you are breathing in the guilt of all the RFMs all over the world. Then breathe out love. See what happens.

- ✤ Get inspired by following Bill Moyers online at billmoyers.com. The guests he interviews will give you hope. In addition to covering politics, he addresses issues of racism, economic inequality, gun control, climate change, and much more.

- ✤ Use your privilege as an opportunity to serve. Realize that if you had to work to find food or shelter, you would not have the energy to contribute. Because your basic needs are met, you can find your ways to be of service.

- ✤ If you are particularly interested in environmental work, join primatologist and anthropologist Jane Goodall's organization at janegoodall.org.

- ✤ Remember that you cannot save all of the people, animals, and plants that are suffering. Feel the love that is in your heart and send it out whenever you run into someone or something which needs it. Use your particular religious or spiritual beliefs to send out a prayer or a blessing.

- ✤ Read the following list of contradictory fears. Take time to think about which ones apply to you and write about them in your journal. These fears may get in the way of your taking action in the world. Keep in mind that as you work through this book, many of these fears will be explained. Recognizing and acknowledging your fears can be the first step in finding freedom from them.

Failure/Success
Losing/Winning
Belonging/Not belonging
Change/Stagnation

Criticism/Praise
Boredom/Challenge
Reaching your potential/Falling short
Being normal/Not being normal
Low expectations/High expectations
Deciding/Indecisiveness
Mediocrity/Excellence
Disappointing others/Pleasing others

- Read the book *Trauma Stewardship: An Everyday Guide to Caring for Self While Caring for Others*, by Lipsky and Burk, if you are working in a field that requires frequent contact with trauma or if you need help coping with what you see in the news media.

- Find inspiring people and projects at TED.com.

- Discover your life purpose(s) and live it (them). Contribute in your unique voice through your passions. Use multiple methods to figure out what to do including psychotherapy, information interviews, travel, apprenticing, shadowing, schooling, mindfulness, astrology, religious retreats, and vision quests.

- If you start to ruminate, remember that worrying will not help. Instead, distract yourself with an activity that needs your total focus, such as painting, biking, computer programming, yoga, prayer, cooking, skateboarding, or playing music. This can disrupt the pattern and move you back into balance.

- Read Bill Plotkin's book, *Wild Mind,* and attend one of his wilderness treks. Find him at animas.org.

- Make sure that you have experiences that allow you to be physically touched in loving ways. If no humans are currently available, find a friendly cat or a loyal dog to supply the necessary contact.

❧ Notice if you get caught in negative thinking loops about yourself that stop you from taking action. If you are stuck in self-criticism, make a list of all of those negative thoughts. Then, make a second list opposite each thought that is the actual truth. For example, you might be telling yourself, "Nothing I do is ever good enough." The truth might be, "My standards are often so high that I don't reach my goals. But, in fact, when I look closely at what I produce, it's often quite substantial and creative." Keep your list handy so that you can reread your truths when you are tempted to slip into self-deprecation.

❧ Let yourself take breaks now and then. Go into temporary denial about your own problems and those of the world. Just have fun!

❧ Remember that, like the rain forest, you can make a significant contribution to the planet when you are living your authentic life.

Chapter Three

Perfectionism, Precision, Procrastination

I've missed more than 9,000 shots in my career. I've lost almost 300 games…I've failed over and over and over again in my life—and that is why I succeed.
~Michael Jordan[29]

Extrinsic Perfectionism

RFMs experience two particular brands of perfectionism. See if any of the statements below apply to you.

- You were over-praised for your accomplishments when you were young.
- You came to believe that you were loved because of your achievements.
- You felt that you had to live up to expectations that you were smart, so as not to disappoint others or yourself.
- If you make even a simple mistake, you feel like a failure.
- If you make a mistake, it proves you are not as smart as others think, and that is a frightening thought.
- You are used to learning things quickly, so you do not want to risk trying something you might not excel at immediately.

- Schoolwork was easy, so you could procrastinate until the very last minute and still get an A. Now, you do not know how *not* to procrastinate.
- If you procrastinate, you blame your end product on "not enough time" because you do not want people to know you are not as smart as they say you are and so that you do not risk a negative evaluation of something you have put your heart into.

The items on this list are experiences of what I call "extrinsic perfectionism," sometimes referred to as unhealthy, neurotic, or maladaptive perfectionism. It is an externally learned perfectionism that develops in childhood. Anyone can acquire this type of perfectionism. It is usually the result of growing up in a dysfunctional family where you felt inadequate in some way. Simply stated, you decided that if you could just be perfect, your parents would love you. But it has additional elements if you are an RFM.[30]

Extrinsic perfectionism is an unhealthy need to be right, be the best, and not make mistakes as a way to prove you are worthy of love. With this perfectionism, you put pressure on yourself to achieve at the highest levels at all times. Even small errors feel like failures. And failure equals worthlessness.

Interestingly, RFMs do not need a dysfunctional family to be perfectionists. If your precociousness was overly praised by parents, teachers, or relatives, or if there was an overemphasis on grades or performance, you may have concluded that your value as a human depended on your achievement. Making simple mistakes, then, can be a threat to your very personhood.

When you were a young child, you probably learned skills earlier than most youngsters. This may have caused the adults in your life to pay extra attention and, perhaps, remark excessively about your intelligence and your accomplishments. You also might not have experienced as much trial and error in early developmental tasks, so you did not experience a learning process that included lots of falling down and getting back up again.[31] Over time, this set up a dependency on ease of learning and praise, coupled with a belief that you were loved for your accomplishments. Thus, your sense of self is built upon a foundation of pressure to achieve and achieve easily.[32]

Eleanor, a curly-haired client in her 20s, described her need for approval as an "addiction." She said she received so much praise for achievement as a child that she had grown dependent on it. She had been the "teacher's pet" and now, as an adult, she watched herself desperately seek affirmation from her new boss. Her behavior appalled her, but she did not know how to curtail it.

Another client, Michelle, described her pattern of quitting if she found that she did not learn something easily. She said that she had natural talent for soccer and at one point moved to the position of goalie where she was successful fairly quickly. Then, as she needed to learn more to improve her skills, she hit that awkward stage where she had to practice the new techniques before she would be good at them. At that point, she quit.

Like Michelle, you may not give yourself time to practice new skills. You may not realize that most people need lots of practice to master something. Yet, when you do not find learning easy, you are uncomfortable and confused.

Procrastination

Extrinsic perfectionism, then, often leads to procrastination because of the pressure to be perfect. Procrastination becomes a way to reduce this pressure and avoid disappointing yourself and others. You may say to yourself, "If I do it the night before it's due and it's not great, it's because I didn't have the time." So, you end up waiting until the last minute to complete a task.

Most of the time, you can still produce something of quality, even in a short span of time, which only serves to complicate matters. In fact, I wonder if this ability to produce quality quickly is the main reason so many RFMs fall into the procrastination trap.

Procrastination patterns can start in school with assignments that are not challenging. You can complete an assignment the night before it is due and still get an A. Waiting to complete an assignment until the last minute becomes reinforced by a school system that does not motivate its brightest students.

Once perfectionism and procrastination have been in place for years, the behaviors and beliefs are hard to change. In Jane Burka and Lenora Yuen's book, *Procrastination*, they explain:

> *Confronting and changing long-held assumptions about you and your family can be unnerving and disorienting. This is why procrastination is so hard to overcome. It's not simply a matter of changing a habit; it requires changing your inner world. However, as you access capabilities and parts of yourself that have been held back by procrastination, you can derive great pleasure in claiming your whole self. This integration is the true basis for self-esteem.*[33]

Other factors are at play in the complicated and contradictory world of perfectionism and procrastination. RFMs often find themselves enormously frustrated with basic, repetitive tasks. Consciously or unconsciously you might think, "What I'm doing is so mundane, I can at least make it more interesting by adding time pressure." The urgency produced by the time limit makes the assignment more intellectually appealing.

In other situations, RFMs find straightforward tasks to be anything but. When essayist and naturalist Diane Ackerman failed Logic in college, she described how a basic syllogism such as "Johnny has a bat. All bats are blue. What color is Johnny's bat?" would turn into:

> *Blue is traditionally the color of sadness, the Virgin Mary, the sky—maybe he'd prefer a color that better reflects his mood or goals. I've noticed that shadows really aren't black, they're blue. Would he want a bat the color of a shadow? Blue is a color easily*

affected by changing light. . . . What sort of blue is it, anyway—
pearly, sapphire, luminescent?

She concludes, "I was altogether too strange to pass Logic."[34]

In other words, you thrive on activities that make you think outside the box. Or you get better grades in the harder classes because you are more engaged. You can get an A in the organic chemistry class, and yet you wither when you are asked to learn something you already know or to do something rote; you get a D in English 101 because you've known the basics for years. It is hard for others to understand how "if you're so smart," why you do not do everything easily, quickly, and thoroughly.

Have you ever thought to yourself, "I can't be mediocre (ordinary, work hard, ask for help, lose)"? These beliefs also contribute to perfectionism and can be the outcome, again, of growing up in an environment that overemphasized your intellect and achievements. It happens naturally when well-meaning parents, relatives, teachers, and counselors are impressed by your unusually advanced abilities.

Adjusting Expectations

While early praise and expectations to be smart set up a need to be the best, there is also an expectation that learning will be easy. After all, you probably grasp many new ideas and difficult concepts without too much trouble. When this becomes a pattern, then you often do not learn how to struggle with a problem or how to deal with frustration. So, you may find it hard to take risks with activities where you are not guaranteed success because academic success is what you have come to expect from yourself. It is another paradox: You yearn for intellectual challenge while simultaneously fearing it. If you do not succeed, it will prove what you have known all along, that you are an "impostor."[35] In fact, what you need to learn is that your worth is not dependent on how smart you are or how much you achieve, and that substantive learning often requires time, struggle, mistakes, and failure.

This "impostor phenomenon"[36] is more common than you might think. You may feel pressure to be the brightest person in all situations, but underneath that façade lurks the fear of being found out that you are not so smart, after all.

Scott was a grad student who excelled all through public school in academics, sports, and art, but then entered a highly competitive architecture program in college. He had an extremely hard time coping with the experience of being one of several smart kids and felt overwhelmed and anxious most of the time. If he had had early experiences with mental challenges and intellectual peers and learned how to approach difficult situations, he would have been better equipped to handle the greater rigors of college.

Another client, Chris, came to see me because of anxiety in college. She had never learned how to study because schoolwork had been so easy for her. She did not realize that success required effort, mistakes, and failures. When she entered a rigorous science program, she panicked. She was no longer the best student. She had to learn the steps she needed to take to complete an assignment. I had to convince her that she was still smart and to encourage her to let go of having to be the best. She said, "It's crushing. It's so hard to shake. It'll all become abundantly clear: This person is a failure."

Recent research about gene expression and brain plasticity can help ease the pressures associated with perfectionism. Both author David Shenk and journalist Geoff Colvin emphasize that intelligence is not a fixed phenomenon. In fact, Shenk entitled the second chapter of his book *The Genius is All of Us*, "Intelligence is a Process, not a Thing."[37] If you imagine that intelligence is not fixed but rather grows with effort, persistence, and—yes—failure, you might be able to relax your all-or-nothing thinking and move into what Stanford psychology professor Carol Dweck calls a "growth mindset."[38] Even if you were born with a rainforest mind, being smart is not an either/or proposition—particularly where advanced achievement is concerned. Study, practice, effort, risk-taking, mistakes, and more practice are all necessary. In my opinion, Shenk and Colvin are talking more about achievement than intellect, but their theories can be helpful when working with perfectionism. I do believe that Dweck's theory has been misinterpreted by some, and as I understand it and explain it to clients, I have found that it helped ease the pressure to be perfect.

Asking for help can be another challenge if you feel that you are supposed to know all of the answers. How can you need aid when you are the one everyone else goes to? You may have looked for help, but have found it to be inadequate. You might even have more skills than someone you hire who is a known expert in that field. This can be frustrating and discouraging. Barbara Kerr, counseling psychology professor at University of Kansas, explains:

> Gifted individuals are used to authorities who are not as bright as they are, and they often despair of ever finding a helper who can speak their language and match their enthusiasm measure for measure. They become cynical and resistant to helpers, having too much experience with teachers and counselors who just do not or will not understand them.[39]

Fear of Success

Fear of success can also impact perfectionism. If you have been teased for your "braininess" over the years or told to "dumb down," then you may be hiding your talent and minimizing your abilities in order to fit in and be accepted. On an unconscious level, you may still want to please your parents by staying small or contained or invisible if, at an early age, you felt their discomfort with your curiosity. If you have felt jealousy from parents, siblings, friends, teachers, or others, you may believe that you will hurt them by being all that you are. Consequently, you do not stretch as far as you can.

What is odd is that you may feel both the pressure to achieve and the need to hide your achievements and abilities. No wonder it is hard to understand and explain your experience.

Phyllis, a sweet client in her 50s, spoke about a pattern of hiding her light and downplaying awards she received when she was in school. Certainly, bragging is inappropriate and can be destructive. We have all known people we avoid because they seem so impressed with themselves. But we also know that those folks likely need to boast because of their insecurities. By contrast, RFMs tend to overcompensate by shrinking. Phyllis told me that she had not even included all of her strengths in her resume because it was so hard to acknowledge her many accomplishments.

Understand the difference between boasting about your achievements and living your fullest life. Even if you surpass your parents or your mentors, even if others are uncomfortable, it is important that you step into your wholeness.

You might end up not only hiding your abilities, but avoiding success because of the pressure that can come with it. Once you are seen as accomplished, there is often an expectation that you will always perform in an exemplary manner. That pressure may be just too much to bear.

Having to measure up to past achievements, though, may be something you feel from others. It may be real. It may not be. But to avoid that real or imagined pressure, you stay small. And if your identity is entangled with your achievement, it can be easier to underperform than face the pressure of praise and the risk of failure. As Burka and Yuen explain, "[Y]ou worry success will create a sense of helplessness instead of a sense of power; you will no longer be yourself, you will turn into someone you don't like, and you won't be able to keep this alien 'you' from taking over."[40]

In *The War of Art*, author Steven Pressfield adds:

We know that if we embrace our ideals, we must prove worthy of them. And that scares the hell out of us. What will become of us? We will lose our friends and family, who will no longer recognize us. We will wind up alone, in the cold void of starry space, with nothing and no one to hold on to.

Of course this is exactly what happens. But here's the trick. We wind up in space, but not alone. Instead, we are tapped into an unquenchable, undepletable, inexhaustible source of wisdom, consciousness, companionship. Yeah, we lose friends. But we find friends, too, in places we never thought to look. And they're better friends, truer friends. And we're better and truer to them.[41]

Bill Plotkin explains the fear of living to our fullest this way:

We long to discover the secrets and mysteries of our individual lives, to find our unique way of belonging to this world, to recover the never-before-seen treasure we were born to bring to our communities. . . . Alongside our greatest longing lives an equally great terror of finding the very thing we seek. Somehow we know that doing so will irreversibly shake up our lives, our sense of security, change our relationship to everything we hold as familiar and dear. But we also suspect that saying no to our deepest desires will mean self-imprisonment in a life too small.[42]

Intrinsic Perfectionism

Another type of perfectionism, which I call "intrinsic," is also known as healthy, positive, or adaptive perfectionism.[43] Intrinsic perfectionists:

- Strive for beauty, balance, harmony, justice, and precision in all things.
- Are often idealistic and have exceedingly high expectations and standards for themselves and others.
- Were thought of as lazy or obstinate in school but were actually struggling with their desire for depth, comprehensiveness, and accuracy.
- Could get an A on a school assignment, though if it was not up to their standards, they were not satisfied.

These qualities are innate in every RFM I have ever met. That deep soulful desire for beauty, balance, harmony, and precision is at the root of true quality and what produces great symphonies, cathedrals, surgeries, and iPhones. It is why you can be moved to tears when the light hits the leaves just right at dusk. And it can be the reason you are researching into the night or cannot finish a project because there is much more to discover, and more to taste, see, hear, smell, and understand. Your standards are exceptionally high.

Others can label your expectations unrealistic, but it is not that simple. You have a vision of what is possible and you ache to achieve it. Because of your unusual capacity for production, when you are motivated, you can create at a very high level. But you may never feel satisfied because you strive for perfection. You keep raising the bar.[44]

You might feel obsessed or driven when it comes to creating or learning. You have to meet an "inner agenda."[45] This can look dysfunctional to others, but it is not. I remember a friend of mine who used to say when she got particularly engrossed in a project, that she was in her "overs" and that she needed to slow down and do less. But she was actually manifesting her vision and from this she was able to produce extraordinary work. She was also accused of being too critical of herself and others, when, in fact, she was making astute, thoughtful observations.

Intrinsic perfectionism can be hard to understand because it can look like extrinsic perfectionism. It can also mean that certain rote obligations get neglected or put on the back burner or that work does not get completed—a way of being that looks nothing like perfection. As a result, you might have to work hard to prioritize projects so that you do not fail a class or lose a job.

This does not just apply to large projects. You might have to create the perfect meatloaf or the precisely choreographed exercise routine. Or, as my client Gary shared, "I spent an hour and a half on a three-sentence email. I had to make it long before I could make it short. I still don't think it's right."

But you are likely to always need to aim for beauty, balance, harmony, justice, and precision, because that is what feeds your soul and makes your heart soar. Once you understand it, you will need to find ways to accommodate the mundane, necessary paperwork of life, because if you land in jail for, say, tax evasion, it will be hard to concentrate on the latest photos from the Mars Rover. Seriously, once RFMs realize that they do not need to give up being obsessed, they are able to take breaks for the necessary details of human functioning.

Interestingly, Shenk describes a scenario I see quite often as part of intrinsic perfectionism.

> *Deliberate practice requires a mind-set of never, ever, being satisfied with your current ability. It requires a constant self-critique, a pathological restlessness, a passion to aim consistently just beyond one's capability so that daily disappointment and failure is actually desired, and a never-ending resolve to dust oneself off and try again and again and again.*[46]

In the case of the RFM, I would not say that failure is preferred; in fact, it is often feared. The restlessness is strong but not pathological. And yet, the striving, the vision, the obsession with beauty in its largest sense, is ongoing.

As Linda Silverman, Director of the Gifted Development Center in Denver, explains:

> *Perfectionism is a component of the drive for self-actualization . . . The gifted Self envisions what could be instead of just what is, it longs to bring that vision into reality, and, often, it is capable of realizing its dreams.*[47]

Or, as Mary-Elaine Jacobsen suggests, "What looks like a neurotic obsessive-compulsive trait may instead be the manifestation of the Herculean work and perseverance inherent in the process of self-actualization."[48] She adds that dissatisfaction, impatience and continual striving are not neurotic when seen in this context.

This discontent exists because of your high standards and also because of your need for novelty and stimulation. It is like the athlete who must work out every day. If you do not get your intellectual exercise, which includes opportunities for expression and expansion, your "muscles" may start to atrophy and your mood may plummet to the point of serious depression. Standards, expectations, and necessity all contribute to this type of inborn perfectionism.

Intrinsic perfectionism may be the most misunderstood aspect of this very complicated phenomenon. And yet, on a very good day, it may be the source of your greatest satisfaction.

Gina: She's so Smart, She'll be Fine

Gina, 24, a red-headed Texan, came to see me because of struggles with perfectionism, sadness, and loneliness. She was a graduate student with a double major in dance performance and nonprofit management. She told me that it was hard to make friends and trust them due to her intensity, high expectations, and history of losses. She described a complicated extended family, two workaholic educator parents, a history of family counseling, and a troubled brother who received much of the attention.

In many families, the gifted child can be neglected because the assumption is that "she'll be fine, she'll figure it out for herself, and so she doesn't need help." When Gina did get attention from her parents, it was for her achievements. This was the set-up for her extrinsic perfectionism. She wrote:

> *My grades became an obsession for me, and I worked to get straight A's in everything. I barely slept, staying up late to muscle through piles of homework. Panic attacks started when I was a junior in high school and the college search ramped up. I didn't have much of a social life, spending my nights doing homework and my weekends doing extracurricular activities to make my college applications look better.*

Gina had much more experience than her fellow college students in both dance performance and in nonprofit management. She felt their resentment when she would share what she knew, trying to be helpful. An extravert who was driven to learn and achieve at the highest levels, she often felt let down by friends, who became tired of interacting long before she did. Some of her college professors did not match her high standards. She described anger and frustration at not being seen, having to hold herself back, and getting inadequate intellectual stimulation. She said, "I'm constantly tempering my perfect expectations to actually exist in this imperfect world. It is a constant negotiation with myself in all areas of my life."

Gina expected that in college she would have academic freedom and support for her intellectual enthusiasm. Unfortunately, this was rarely the case. She ran into rigid, outdated teaching techniques and professors intimidated by her experience and questions. Instead of embracing her intense curiosity, teachers asked her—both directly and indirectly—to slow down, "dumb down," and help other students who were less motivated. "I need someone to mentor me in a meaningful way but I'm five steps ahead of everyone," she sighed.

Gina had a serious problem with procrastination. She would put off major college assignments until the night before they were due. Yet, she was driven to get straight A's and her parents accepted nothing less. Even though she felt enormous pressure to achieve, she was paralyzed by a fear of failure. She explained, "I have to fight so hard to prove myself. I get defensive and don't trust myself . . . I need emotional support but I hate being vulnerable. It's a sign of weakness."

She couldn't begin work until she felt she had to. Gina's success with grades and her skills in communication hid her anxiety, which showed up in her many physical symptoms: migraines, TMJ, and chronic pain from injuries that had yet to heal completely. She was seeing a naturopath, a massage therapist, and an acupuncturist who were addressing some of those issues.

Limitless

Gina said that she procrastinated via mindless activities so she would not feel her loneliness and other painful emotions. She compared her life experience to that of the main character in the movie *Limitless*, who takes a drug that facilitates the use of all of his brain capacity and, in doing so, creates chaos.

Like many cases with gifted adults, this one was complex. It included understanding the challenges of the RFM, particularly perfectionism; complicated dysfunctional family dynamics; and physical/sexual assaults by a former boyfriend. Being understood and accepted as a gifted person was where we began. As with all of my clients, Gina took the RFM quiz, read articles, and asked me questions. Even though she had always been a high achiever, she doubted her giftedness.

We looked at ways that Gina could reduce her stress and her physical tension through activities such as yoga, massage, walks in nature, and healthier eating habits, and then made a list of these options for her to have handy. As we began to move more deeply into the reasons for her perfectionism and procrastination, we identified Gina's link between her sense of worth and her achievements and her resulting extreme fear of failure and misunderstanding of what failure actually is. Related issues included her need to have something in her life she could control, and the need to create more intellectual excitement.

Gina described a problematic relationship with her parents. In particular, her mother sounded absorbed in her work and like a poor communicator. Gina said that when she and her mother disagreed, her mother could not admit any fault. Interactions were frustrating and demoralizing. She explained, "I don't feel heard or emotionally safe. She's overbearing and never wrong. My feelings aren't valid." Even so, Gina hoped she could build a satisfying connection with her mother. Gina had lost her two closest friends after moving from her hometown for college and felt bereft about the possibility of not being able to turn to her parents for support. She still held out hope that she could reach her mother and get the attention and love that she deserved.

I suspected that there were deeper layers of emotion that we were not touching, but when I made a move to head that direction, I could see in her body language that it was not the right time. Gina's schedule was packed with school obligations and so heading into a grieving process might have destabilized her. Along with her double major, Gina had a Graduate Teaching Fellowship and was running an office, creating databases, and organizing campus arts performances. As an RFM, she was used to accomplishing quite a bit in a short time but processing trauma is a delicate operation, even for a fast learner.

At the following meeting, Gina voiced concerns about a past intimate relationship with a man whom she felt was the only person who matched her intellectually, who understood her, and with whom she could talk about anything. She provided details of how their relationship had ended and his unresolved childhood issues created "drama" in his life she wanted to avoid. It was an enormous loss. She also told me about a relationship in college with a man who was abusive and began stalking her after the relationship ended.

Clearly, we were moving into more challenging material. For the first time, Gina was able to tap into her emotions around these relationships and let down some of her guard with me. I could also tell that at this stage it would be counter-productive to push her to share her fears and her grief. Even though Gina could move through intellectual material at lightning speed, emotional processing of trauma needs careful pacing.

After meeting for several sessions, Gina reported that she had seen progress on a few fronts. She had felt dissatisfied with two of her classes and made appointments with both professors. She and I made a plan for these meetings so that she might communicate in a way that would be most effective, while suggesting ways that both professors could better meet her needs. She was pleasantly surprised by the results. One professor agreed to set up an independent study project so she would not have to sit through the class. The other did not change the course, but he did acknowledge his appreciation of her abilities and mistakes he had made in designing the class. This was a start and Gina felt some satisfaction.

With her mother, Gina set up a phone conversation with some specific parameters so that she was not the child who had to listen to her parent's demands, but rather the adult making clear statements about what she needed from her mother. To Gina's surprise, her mother admitted errors she had made and agreed to pay closer attention to her daughter's interests and needs. Gina felt relieved and hopeful.

Pump the Brakes

Gina even reported progress with procrastination. She had found some ways to structure her time, organize work in smaller chunks, and reduce the pressure she placed on herself. Gina continued to grapple with perfectionism, but now that she understood that her standards were much higher than her peers' and professors', she was able to ease up on the amount and quality of work she expected of herself. She was able to let less important projects be merely excellent, rather than perfect. She still claimed, "I need to be perfect at all times at everything," but we had made a start.

Gina continued to struggle to find friends. She said she learned to "pump the brakes" at times to allow others to keep up with her. But often, that was not enough. Gina had strong opinions and readily voiced them. She was deeply concerned about politics and issues of justice and equality. She was both fierce in her beliefs and, at the same time, soft-hearted and easily hurt. Potential friends did not stick around for long.

Even with the challenges she faced, at the end of the school year, Gina designed a unique final recital for her dance performance degree that demonstrated her large range of interests and depth of knowledge. I attended the performance. It was apparent to me that something extraordinary was taking place on stage. This was intrinsic perfectionism at its best.

Gina came to a session after a three-day weekend training with a Dao community, a spiritual philosophy that she had been studying for some time. Glowing with enthusiasm, she told me that she was "transformed" and described what sounded like a profound spiritual awakening. In particular, Gina was able to release some of the enormous anger that had built up from years of misunderstandings, assaults, losses, and disappointments. I hoped that developing this spiritual connection could help Gina continue to ease up on herself and reduce the pressure to always be perfect. Happily, she also reported meeting people she could relate to who might become friends, particularly two professional women in their 40s.

I heard again from Gina after she returned from a summer of travel and we met for several more sessions. She was greatly influenced by the people she had met and family members she had visited abroad. She expressed concerns about how to create a future that allowed her to contribute to a better world, tapping into a larger spirituality and not participating in what she described as "a corrupt system run by corporate interests." She was rethinking whether to get a job with an organization for the security of income and benefits or to strike out on her own as a consultant and world traveler.

Gina had already made contacts with an international nonprofit organization working with children and the arts, and she had other ideas as well. I suspected that she could combine her entrepreneurial skills with her computer knowledge, her dance training, and her swift learning capacity in many areas to build a successful consulting business upon graduation.

I hoped that Gina would continue to access counseling and other complementary medical modalities as she built her life path. She needed to access multiple forms of support to accommodate her sensitivities and complexity. As our counseling relationship drew to a close, Gina shared that she had built a clearer self-accepting picture of who she was as a person with a rainforest mind. She appreciated the beauty of her intrinsic perfectionism. She acknowledged that her understanding of the roots of procrastination had helped her gain some control over it. She was gentler with herself and while she still had the highest standards, her drive to achieve at all costs had softened.

At the same time, Gina was still grappling with whether to be a part of a system that she felt was unjust and corrupt. Her vision of perfection made it even harder to live with hypocrisy and injustice. She had a huge capacity for deep mental, emotional, and spiritual awareness. But even though she could hear the chainsaws in the distance, she would continue to stand tall. She would make her mark. I was sure of that.

Diane: Terrified of Mediocrity

Diane, 33, had large, dark, questioning brown eyes. She said that she wanted to be "more successful" and reach her "unrealized potential," but that she struggled with low self-esteem and considerable self-doubt. Even though she had been identified for gifted programs since elementary school, she found college difficult and took ten years to get her BA in fine arts, with a final GPA of 2.85.

Diane said she had been depressed in college and found it hard to focus or finish assignments. She said that she had interests in "everything" and a "filtering problem" and wondered if she might have ADD. Public school had been easy academically, but difficult socially. She said she was shy and had been teased by the other children.

In an early session, Diane, dressed in black slacks and a dark turtleneck sweater, described symptoms of perfectionism. An avid reader from age four, she completed work quickly and spent time waiting for her peers to catch up. She said she never really learned study skills or how to take steps to solve difficult problems. As a result, she now avoided anything that she suspected she could not complete quickly. Because her identity had been formed around praise for easy answers and good grades, her sense of worth was threatened when she did not achieve at an exceptional level. This is likely where her perfectionism started. She said, "I expect to understand things immediately. If I don't, I'm extremely uncomfortable and I just

abandon whatever it is. I'm terrified of mediocrity or of being average."
College, then, had been confusing, demoralizing, and depressing.

Even with her difficult college experiences and her fear of risking something new, Diane had started her own website in an online marketplace where she sold odd found objects that people would use for their creative projects. In spite of her organizational and focusing limitations, she had created a somewhat successful part-time business. We were not sure if she had ADD, but often, when an RFM has a learning disability, they are high functioning enough to compensate for the disorder, which may have been true for Diane. The RFM looks more average due to the learning problem, but once the disorder is addressed, functioning can increase to higher levels.

Barraged by Thoughts and Images

Being easily overwhelmed and distracted, Diane said she loved noticing unusual patterns and textures and differences in light. Because she was able to find connections between disparate ideas and objects and because of the unending resources on the internet, she felt barraged with thoughts and images. This kept her from taking concrete steps to completing projects.

One of our goals in counseling was to determine if this distractibility was due to a highly creative mind, ADD, or some combination of the two. Because she had great difficulty with time management, planning, and organization, I referred her to a specialist in ADD for an evaluation. I have encountered some clients who have been misdiagnosed with ADD or ADHD, often as children, but Diane's number and type of symptoms made the diagnosis more probable. She made an appointment and had a thorough battery of tests which indicated a moderate level of ADD. The psychologist recommended medication and neurofeedback, both of which she agreed to try.

Diane was in the process of applying to online graduate programs for a degree in information science when I started seeing her, and she began a program while in counseling. Though this brought her back up against her academic fears and failures, she was staying on top of her assignments and getting her work in on time. A couple of months after starting the program, however, she dropped out, stating that she had decided that information science was not, in fact, what she thought it was and that she could not see herself benefiting from the coursework. She also was frustrated by the material, since she was not learning anything new. I wondered whether the perfectionist in her had influenced her decision.

Muddled and Flustered

We spent some time comparing traits of the RFM with ADD behaviors. Diane said that she had great difficulty with transitions, changing momentum, and being interrupted once she got started on something. She explained that her brain was "frayed, frazzled, scrambling, and drifting."

Because she felt so "muddled and flustered" during interruptions, Diane said that she needed to be quite methodical and routine-oriented to get things done or even to remember a list of items. She said that she did accomplish more when she took her medication. Previously, even a task as simple as picking something off the floor would normally be postponed, but with the medicine, she would pick it up easily. She said that lots of times it was as though her wheels were spinning, her car in gear but not moving. She described a need for "scaffolding" and help "finding [her] footing."

I told Diane that RFMs could be immersion learners, plunging deeply into a topic and not wanting to come out until they learned everything they could. During a "flow" state, RFMs lose track of time and space and find it hard to return to ordinary reality. Nonetheless, I believed that Diane's extreme degree of difficulty with change was due to ADD. The way she described her improved ability to accomplish tasks when taking the medication also seemed pretty compelling.

When it came to having sky-high standards and expectations and not turning in work because it was not good enough, I told Diane this was likely the perfectionism of the RFM. When she told me that she did not want to participate in the world because of human destructiveness and exploitation, I told her that this was likely the existential depression of the RFM. When she said she was conflicted about whether to write exactly what she wanted for her blog about creative reuse of materials or water it down to reach a larger audience, I told her this was a typical dilemma for the RFM. My suggestion was that she ought to write it from her genuine, fully-engaged self, as this would be more satisfying for her and she would likely find an appropriate following if she spoke from her authentic voice.

In continuing to examine Diane's concerns about a future career, we started to think about the benefits and challenges of introversion. Even though she said that she preferred a classroom to an online class, it became clear that Diane much preferred solitude. This was another way Diane felt different and abnormal. I suggested that she read the recent literature on introversion, such as Susan Cain's research, which talks about its many benefits. Diane described a sister and sister-in-law who were both extroverts and her sense of being out of sync. She said she liked exploring cities and alleyways on her own, not for the people but for the "visual feast."

Apologies for Accelerating

Diane told me that she felt apologetic about "accelerating past others," referring especially to her relationship with her parents. An RFM may be underachieving for this reason. As I explained to Diane, a fear of success can result from not wanting to grow past your parents, friends, and even your mentors. Her challenge, then, was how to support her aging parents without staying stuck in their world. Understanding the issues and allowing her emotions to flow was a good beginning.

She also read more about executive function problems as a way to continue to sort out the causes of her difficulties. RFMs commonly find themselves doing their own research to answer their questions. Practitioners, including myself, are often not as bright as the RFM, which can lead to frustration with supposed experts who may not know as much as the client.

Diane was researching depression, dysthymia, antidepressant medications, and dopamine impacts on mood and concentration to see if she could find some answers. I referred her to a psychiatric nurse practitioner who had experience with ADD. On her recommendation, Diane decided to try medication for the symptoms of depression while continuing to see if neurofeedback would produce results. We talked about how she needed a team of practitioners because of her complexity and how no one person would be able to find the answer for her. Though frustrating, this is the normal reality for RFMs.

I began to read more about ADD and found the books by Edward M. Hallowell to be particularly helpful. He said that working with ADD is a lifelong challenge and that it is important to use a multidimensional approach while maintaining a sense of humor. Hallowell strongly suggested medication and explained that depression often comes with ADD.[49] As I educated myself about ADD, I could more confidently help Diane accept the diagnosis rather than label herself lazy. In one session, she described her struggle with ADD like trying to "wrangle a pile of wriggling snakes, reaching into the pile as the snakes slither all over each other, grabbing one, then attempting to straighten it out." Imagine the combination of perfectionism and ADD. Normally, extremely high standards and needs for precision create significant frustration. If, however, you aim for perfection while holding a bunch of gyrating snakes, well, chances are the reptiles will win.

But Diane did not give up. Happily, she came to a session a few months later telling me that her "gears were working together" and that she felt "at home in her skin" and even confident. Just in time. Diane had plans to move to another part of the country with her partner as he pursued his PhD. Diane said that she felt able to accomplish tasks more easily and less pressure to produce perfection. At the same time, she could appreciate her intrinsic perfectionism as she carefully designed improvements for her website. She reported feeling more self-accepting in general and looked forward to expanding her online shop and starting a blog. She was ready to express the many ideas she had tumbling around in her "not-so-frazzled-anymore" brain.

Strategies

- Keep your high standards and high ideals. Yes, keep them and love them. Just try not to expect others to have them. You may want to find other RFMs who are as particular as you to share feedback which will have more meaning and value.

- Even though your intrinsic perfectionism can lead you to true greatness, quality results, and maybe even human evolution, try modifying it at times when exquisiteness and transformation are not at stake. Consider that not everything you do has to be so thorough and precise. Does every email really need perfect punctuation? Choose the projects that you want to be pristine and let others be shallow and surface. They will still probably be excellent. Yes, you can have excellence without perfection. And you may manage to get more done.

- Strive for wholeness and balance instead of perfection.

- If you have difficulty with mundane tasks such as paperwork or record-keeping, get help setting up a system that organizes your calendar, your office, and/or your necessary tasks. This will save time so that you can get back to what you love. If this seems extremely difficult, hire a coach, a secretary, or a professional organizer. If you keep putting it off, and if time management and organization feel impossible, consider getting an assessment for ADD.

- For more information on ADD and other twice-exceptionalities, read *Bright Not Broken*, by Diane Kennedy and Rebecca Banks.

- Practice allowing mistakes (especially if you are a parent). A mistake is not the same as failure.

❧ You can learn more from failure than from success. Some great inventions were the result of great failures. As Thomas Edison said, "I have not failed. I have successfully discovered 1,200 ideas that don't work."

❧ Failures make great stories for holiday gatherings, memoirs, TED talks, and comedy routines.

❧ Put more emphasis on the process than the product. Most of your life is spent on the journey, not at the destination. Practice measuring your success by factors other than the "grade." What about effort, enjoyment, complexity, opportunities for growth, learning something new, or meeting new people?

❧ Break down projects into smaller parts. Make a list of the specific steps you need to take. Set a minimal goal and give yourself 15 minutes to work on it. Expect setbacks. Give yourself small rewards for progress.

❧ An inspiring quick read that will help you find your muse and conquer your resistance is *The War of Art*, by Steven Pressfield.

❧ Work on developing a "growth mindset" instead of a "fixed mindset." These are concepts presented by Carol Dweck in her book, *Mindset*. She suggests that you need to approach life as a learner who can always change and grow, as opposed to someone who believes that their personality and intelligence are "carved in stone." Mistakes will cease to be failures or statements of your worthlessness, and instead become opportunities for discovery. Dweck also observes that working at something strengthens your brain. As you learn something that you did not know before, new synaptic connections will form. So, when something is difficult and you are uncomfortable with the struggle, remind yourself that you are upgrading your brain. Even though there is controversy over some of Dweck's concepts, you can benefit from the theory.

❧ If you procrastinate because life is otherwise too slow and mundane, look for ways to get more intellectual stimulation or a new challenge.

❧ If a strident, critical inner voice is constantly berating you, get a journal and begin a series of dialogues with that part of you. Find out why your critic is so persistent. See what feelings and insights come up, and then write about those. Find new ways to satisfy the critic's needs for control, like letting it vent for ten minutes each day and then asking it to back off. See if you can find out how the critic is trying to protect you. Express gratitude for the misguided help, and then offer it another job. Check out books on journal writing by authors such as Christina Baldwin and Kathleen Adams.

❧ If you're uncomfortable with your introversion, read Susan Cain's *Quiet: The Power of Introverts in a World That Can't Stop Talking.*

❧ Your critical voice may be the result of growing up with emotional, sexual, or physical abuse or neglect, or in an alcoholic family. You may need a good therapist to help you work through the impact of your family system.

❧ You may have done a lot of inner work on your own because you have not found professionals who are more capable than you. It can be discouraging to look for a therapist. Do not give up! A good therapist can make a big difference in how you view yourself and in your healing/individuation process. Look for someone comfortable with your speed and intensity, who has done his/her own therapy and is still working on him/herself, who is very bright and highly sensitive, and whose philosophy of counseling appeals to you. Trust your intuition.

❧ Two good books for dealing with impostor syndrome are *Presence*, by Amy Cuddy, and *The Secret Thoughts of Successful Women*, by Valerie Young.

❧ If you are in a pattern of not being able to acknowledge your successes, even to yourself, take some time out to remember one or more experiences when you were proud of yourself. Recall the details of the memory and feel in your body the experience of accomplishment. Breathe in the positive response from others or your own happiness. Maybe you have an image of an audience applauding or a teacher smiling at you. Even as you do not want to depend on your achievements for your self-esteem, you do not have to hide or feel ashamed of them either.

❧ Avoid all-or-nothing thinking, such as believing that a project is either perfect or a failure. Think about the parts that worked well and the parts that did not. One error does not make the entire project a failure.

❧ If you find yourself surpassing your parents, teachers, or mentors in your achievements, let yourself feel the conflict in that, as well as any sadness or loneliness. Give yourself permission to move ahead and look for colleagues or new mentors.

❧ If you tend to imagine the worst outcome in a situation (called "catastrophizing") get logical and decide if it is actually realistic that the worst will really happen. What is a more reasonable result? Can you let go of imagining a terrible outcome? Or, if you need to imagine the worst because you need to feel prepared, can you recognize that the worst is quite unlikely but is a tool you consciously use to keep yourself calmer?

✥ A great resource on perfectionism and procrastination is *Procrastination*, by Burka and Yuen.

✥ Make a list of your own ideas for dealing with procrastination. The following is a partial list from one of my teen clients:

Start early in order to have enough time to stew on it.
Set up an ideal working environment.
Notice when you are distracted and bring yourself back to the task.
Use a timer for work time and break time.
Start by just working for 15 minutes.
Drink enough water. Eat healthful snacks.
Reminders: Every little thing you accomplish is good.
Even though it is not complete, what you have done so far is good.
You do not have to finish, just write another line.
Do not think of the big picture. Do not think about what will follow.
The work is a vehicle for who you want to become.
Negative habits or precedents can be changed.

✥ Remember the words of Steve Jobs in his commencement address at Stanford in 2005:

> *I didn't see it then, but it turned out that getting fired from Apple was the best thing that could have ever happened to me. The heaviness of being successful was replaced by the lightness of being a beginner again, less sure of everything. It freed me to enter one of the most creative periods of my life. . . . Stay hungry. Stay foolish.*[50]

Chapter Four

Too Many Possibilities, Too Many Choices

Career counseling for the gifted needs to be sensitive to their multiple interests, the existential dilemmas they face in making choices, their fear of making an error, their fear of being less than their ideal or not living up to their potential, the depth of their sadness over the road not taken, and their fear that if they try to nurture all their potentials, they will end up second-rate at everything.
~Linda Silverman[51]

Just a Dabbler

If you have so many interests and abilities that you are overwhelmed, embarrassed, frustrated, confused, and very, very busy, chances are you are suffering from multipotentiality.

Signs of multipotentiality include:
- Feeling like a jack-of-all-trades and a master of none
- Feeling like a dilettante
- Changing majors in college many times
- Taking longer to get through college
- Not going to college because you cannot decide on a major
- Having a terrible time choosing one career

- Frequently changing jobs and/or careers
- Being told you can do anything you want (Aren't you lucky?)
- Not feeling lucky

Since you are involved in so many things, you may think you are just a dabbler rather than a person of substance. It is likely, however, that the many projects and careers you begin are by no means shallow but, in fact, quite in-depth. True, you may not finish some of them. If you have learned what you wanted to learn, it may be time to move on even though to someone else it looks as if you did not complete what you started. Perhaps you have not been in a job all that long, yet you have learned the necessary skills, so you find yourself frustrated because you have stopped learning anything new. For many people, mastering the job would be comforting. To you, it may be torture.

Oddly enough, being good at many things can create distress. How do you choose? What do you let go of? Who will cry with you when you choose a medical career over classical piano? Can you do it all?[52]

As Annemarie Roeper observed:

Gifted adults are often confronted with the problem of having too many abilities in too many areas in which they would like to work, discover and excel. For example, university students often move from one field of study to another because they are attracted to both. They may at times end up not doing well in either. However, other gifted students have a great capacity for learning and may be able to study several areas side by side and acquire several doctorates in fields far removed from each other.[53]

Relatives and friends may not understand how hard it is to select just one career path. Or, they may get lost in your high-speed imaginative ruminations about your different choices. They may keep asking you to slow down, quiet down, calm down, and just pick something, anything, for heaven's sake.

Author Margaret Lobenstein uses the label "renaissance soul" to describe this phenomenon. In her book of the same name, she says:

> *Renaissance Souls love nothing better than to take on a new problem or situation and then dig into it . . . until we master the challenge we've set for ourselves. And then, with fresh enthusiasm, we move on to another passion. We are lucky people who, if left to our own devices, are never bored for long.*[54]

As I said, you may or may not feel so lucky.

One client said, "Even though I embraced [my] different activities, for a long time I kept looking for my one true calling. I realized I don't have to pick one thing. I don't have to be a person who lets go of any of my interests."

Barbara Sher, career counselor and author, calls people with this trait "scanners" and describes them as possessing an unending interest in everything and effervescence for life itself. She explains:

> *Scanners want it all, not because they're spoiled but for the same reason all your muscles want exercise. Scanners love variety because they have brains that process things quickly and are ready for new subjects sooner than other people. They have special abilities in many areas, and they're built to use them.*[55]

Sher differentiates between scanners and "divers." The divers choose one thing to examine thoroughly. I would call RFMs diving scanners. They do both.

Choosing and Changing Careers

If you are just starting out in the job market, you may worry that you need to choose one thing and stick with it for life or you will look unreliable. The pressure to specialize is great. It seems that very few universities have interdisciplinary degrees in their graduate programs. In fact, you may know people who have had the same job for 30 years.

But in today's market, many people do change jobs and even career paths multiple times. Career change may be even more important for you. With your ability to learn job skills quickly, you may need to leave a job once you have mastered it and move on to a more challenging position that allows you to learn something new.

How might you do this? If you lose interest in your work after a few years, or if you simply have many career paths you wish to travel, consider moving on to something else. It could be something different within the same organization or a totally new position. Then, show your enthusiasm for the next thing and your confidence in your creativity, flexibility, and depth. Good employers—people you will want to work for—will notice.

Even if employers suspect you will move on in a few years, you can emphasize that the benefits of having you for a short time outweigh the risks of losing you. I am not suggesting that you be irresponsible. Consider the risks and benefits of any changes, particularly when it comes to your financial situation. I am proposing that you may have more options than you realize. Like my multitalented client, Wendy, you might even leave a job (teaching) to try something else (consulting) and then get rehired as a teacher two years later, in the same district, when you realize that you really do want to teach. Wendy was able to make a convincing case and her school district happily took her back. In her book, *Refuse to Choose*, Sher provides many examples of scanners who found innovative ways to do much of what they loved and also earn an income.

When you are at work, it may be hard for you to stay within your job description if you can accomplish your duties easily and quickly. Sandra, an energetic client in her 40s, struggled with this. She explained:

It's hard to know when to say "no" to additional responsibilities because I know I'm capable of doing them. It's also hard to say "no" when I feel like I might be restless or bored if I limit myself only to the job description or the typical expectations of the position.

At the same time, the extra duties were not satisfying and Sandra was not appreciated for doing them. More often than not, her supervisor just took advantage of her willingness to take on more responsibility and her co-workers resented her.

It also may be hard for you to work collaboratively because of your speed, standards, and expectations. Carlos, who was in grad school when I was seeing him, said:

When I take the lead in group settings, my standard of work is always higher than the other people I'm working with. When in a leadership position, I work to make sure all people have a voice and representation in the final product, but the final product is often below a level of standard that I would produce myself. I have learned to give up my high expectations in the interest of good interpersonal communication and positive working relationships.

Perhaps you will consider self-employment. Not only will you have the autonomy that you crave, but will likely have quite a bit of variety to keep you stimulated. Lori, a middle-aged mom, opened a toy store. She loved the challenge of running a business and always having something different to do, including remodeling the building that housed the store. Educating parents about child development and providing quality toys felt like a worthwhile endeavor. Jennifer, an avid bicyclist, owned a children's bookstore. Reading was a passion and she, like Lori, wanted multiple challenges in her daily work and to provide a service to her community. Now Lori is a city planner/landscape architect and Jennifer is writing books on mythology and feminism.

If running a complex business seems overwhelming, consulting might be a good fit. You can teach what you know, serve a broad range of needs, schedule your own time, and work within many different venues.

Of course, if you do not have an entrepreneurial bent, self-employment might not be the right fit for you. You can still work on crafting a career that combines many of your interests and fits a niche in a system that you run. Or you can get a job that meets some of your needs, and then volunteer or explore multiple hobbies.

Antonio, who came to see me because of his overwhelming anxiety, started out in a career in music. He earned a master's degree in piano performance and began teaching. At the same time, he maintained a yoga practice and earned a certificate as an advanced yoga instructor. When those paths were not satisfying, he went back to school for a counseling degree. Now, he is planning to start a counseling practice with a focus on music therapy and trauma, using the latest research on the benefits of yoga for addressing post-traumatic stress disorder. Knowing the particular challenges that musicians face, he has a back-up plan to provide counseling for that population. In his spare time, he studies religion, cooks his wife gourmet meals, and throws pots at a local ceramics studio.

Never too Late

But you may have a job that you cannot leave or you may be stuck in indecision. Jessica, 25, had a well-paying, secure position in admissions at a university. The job provided opportunities to speak to groups, be of service, and travel internationally. Just one more year in the job and she would start to build up a pension. Still, it wasn't enough and, yet, she was terrified of leaving.

Even though she did not know where to focus, Jessica knew she needed to attend graduate school. She wanted greater fulfillment in her career, but could not narrow her interests down to one field. She felt lost and alone in what she described as a "shadowy empty forest that had too many paths that went off far into the foggy distance." She was afraid of choosing the wrong path and was worried that it was too late to make a change, that she had done herself "irreparable damage" by taking the job.

Jessica was interested in public speaking, writing, sociology, humanities, women's issues, literature, theology, math, teaching, politics, law, international relations, medicine, feminism, and becoming a parent. After a session in which I explained multipotentiality, she came to our next appointment saying she had been grieving the loss of "having one calling." She said, "It's shattering to realize that there's not the shining beacon of a single path." In identifying herself as a diving scanner, she was relieved to be able to put a label on what she originally interpreted as doing something wrong or "missing a signal" that would have shown her what to do.

In addition to examining her fears, we talked about ways that Jessica could stay in the job but start to take graduate classes, or how she might volunteer for a nonprofit she respected that needed a public speaker and writer, while keeping her day job. Because she loved writing and research, she imagined a career path similar to Mary Roach, who writes nonfiction on a series of fascinating topics, from human cadavers to space travel. She could find out everything she could about an interest, write about it, talk about it, and then dive into the next interest. I suggested she explore Emilie Wapnick's website, puttylike.com. Emilie coined the word "multipotentialite" and created a community online for support and sharing of ideas.

Jessica was torn between being practical and going for her dreams. She was afraid she was just hoping for some unreachable "pie in the sky." I asked her to consider that pie was available, but she did not have to reach all the way to the sky to get it.

Decisions, Decisions

Along with multiple abilities that make choosing and staying in careers difficult, you may have trouble with decision-making in general. This might be because, as a divergent thinker, you can come up with so many possibilities that you find it difficult to narrow things down and choose one, particularly as you understand how everything is related. Because you are super-sensitive, you are deeply affected by the choices you make. What you choose matters. And because you often consider how other beings will be affected by your choices, you put pressure on yourself to get it right.

In "The Pancake Breakfast," a story in the *New Yorker* by Donald Antrim, his protagonist ruminates:

> *Choice, with its inevitable invitations to loss, is always such a trial. It does not matter, in my experience, that a particular choice consists in apparently unweighty alternatives. Quite the opposite. Choices between banalities are some of our more intimidating ordeals in life.*

He then goes on to describe, in RFM-excruciating detail, how the decision to paint an upstairs room has not been made for years because what begins as a seemingly simple question quickly evolves into "How do I live, knowing that I will one day die and leave you?"[56]

Sound familiar?

Perhaps your need for a specific visual aesthetic means that you take more time than usual deciding on colors for your home: "I tried eight different shades of beige for my living room and observed them in different light for over four months." Or, "In five years, I've painted my living room twelve times." If you are sensitive to color, you may have to do this to be able to feel relaxed in your home. Other people may find this a bit, well, obsessive, but for you, it is normal and, in fact, necessary. Obviously, difficulty with decisions is not just a visual phenomenon. Making choices in any realm can be challenging.

Understanding your multipotentiality, then, can free you up to pursue many of your interests and abilities without guilt or shame. It allows you to use your capacity for creativity in productive ways, instead of finding yourself either paralyzed or overwhelmed. You can design multiple careers and change paths often throughout your adult life. If you choose a path that includes being a stay-at-home parent, be sure to configure ways to drink from a variety of wells so that your child receives a fully nourished you.

Knowing that you take longer to make decisions because you are a divergent thinker, have perfectionist tendencies, are sensitive, and care deeply about your impact, can allow you to dis-identify as a flip-flopper or an obsessive-compulsive, careless, weak time-waster.

Rebecca: Just Pick Something

Twenty-six-year-old grad student Rebecca had soft, deep hazel eyes and straight blonde shoulder-length hair. When she first came into my office looking for help adjusting to grad school, she was dressed comfortably in jeans, T-shirt, and hiking boots. In particular, she said she was dealing with anxiety and lack of confidence, wondering why she felt different from her peers and what to do about it. She said she had counseling when her parents divorced and had found it helpful. Rebecca was majoring in environmental engineering but was unclear about where to head next, what exactly to study, and with whom to work.

Early on, it became clear that Rebecca was dealing with multipotentiality. When trying to choose an area of study during her college career, she had been told repeatedly to "just pick something." But she was capable and interested in so many areas that choosing one thing was nearly impossible. Ruefully, she said, "If I had 20 lives, I wouldn't be able to do everything I wanted to."

Rebecca had started college on a scholarship as a viola performance major but found it to be lonely and impractical, so she switched to mechanical engineering and then to environmental engineering. She also left music because she did not feel that a career in music would have as much of an impact on humanity as science would. Rebecca showed interest and aptitude in debate, chemistry, philosophy, mathematics, business, music, sustainability, and engineering. Any one of these areas could have been the focus of her studies. She also enjoyed reading, researching, gardening, dog agility, and quilting.

In our first sessions, Rebecca described anxiety around teaching classes as a graduate teaching assistant. Her main concern was that she was boring the students. I suggested that most students would find what she was teaching challenging and that she check to find out whether she might, instead, be moving too quickly. She assumed that other students were as capable as she was. This is not uncommon. As an RFM, your abilities are normal for you, so you imagine that others have them as well. Once Rebecca realized this gap, she began to cover the material a bit more slowly. Teaching became easier and more pleasant.

Rebecca was also generally shy around people and lacked confidence. She was tired of shallow conversations and longed for deep connections, but she did not realize that her difficulty with communication might be in part because of her inability to make small talk. When she realized this, she began to feel more relaxed in social situations.

Zen and Obsessed

From an early age, Rebecca was an eager and enthusiastic learner. She recalled loving learning letters on flash cards when she was two years old and listening to her mother read *Lord of the Rings*. She played in a youth orchestra after insisting, at age six, that she take violin lessons. She remembered wanting to learn to play chess, speak Russian because the letters were "so cool," and put together 1,000-piece jigsaw puzzles when she was eight. In eighth grade, she considered becoming a missionary like her grandmother as a way to help others.

Rebecca recalled an independent project she designed in high school. The project involved comparing soil samples next to an oil refinery in a low-income neighborhood with soil in a wealthy neighborhood and then studying public health statistics. She said, "I analyzed lead content in the soil samples and the rate of autism in the area. Lead levels were high in the poor neighborhood. Of course this was not causality but correlation. But I found myself wanting to make policy that would regulate these corporations." This ignited her passion for environmental justice.

We spent most of our early sessions understanding what it meant to have a rainforest mind, particularly multipotentiality, and examining Rebecca's options in her graduate program. She knew that she did not want to focus on one narrow topic. Some sort of interdisciplinary study would be ideal but not easy to design. Rebecca said it was an "ongoing struggle" to decide what career path to follow.

"I struggle with trying to stay with just one field because I'm interested in a lot of different things," she told me.

> *Others often tell me that "you need to focus your interests" or "you must not like to be successful if you leave once you get good at something" or that I'm "flakey." Also sometimes I see connections between things that may not be obvious or important to others. I seem disorganized and unfocused. My problem is I love to learn a job, then I optimize the job to do it in the fastest possible way, then I'm bored, and I want to move on to something else.*

In one session, Rebecca questioned her passion for learning. She wondered if she should try to be "more Zen"—more in the present moment—whether she was walking her dog or gazing at the trees in her neighborhood. When she was involved in personal projects, she found that it would take time to dive in and get into flow, but once immersed, she would not resurface for hours. She was concerned that she was spending too much time alone, although she admitted that she enjoyed the mental gymnastics.

"Immersion learning" is a common learning style for RFMs, and Rebecca's tendency to get engrossed in a subject was not abnormal for an RFM. I suggested she think about how she might allow herself to be both Zen and obsessed at the same time, accepting that research was her version of fun.

At another session, Rebecca described her continuing discomfort when communicating with people, even her fellow students. She reported that when she did try talking with her peers, she felt welcomed, but they did not seem to get her humor. She was thinking of broad, complex concepts during the week, so when her peers asked her what she was working on, she could not come up with a simple straightforward answer. She was not interested in pop culture, either, so this limited her conversational topics.

Interestingly, Rebecca told me about a summer program she had attended at a university a year prior run by an environmental sustainability group. Studying with bright, creative students from around the world, she was in her element. She described a man from Brazil with whom she spoke at such a fast pace that they were speaking over each other, yet they were both just fine with it. Laughing, she recalled that their rapid-fire exchange allowed them to communicate so much more.

Possible Futures

At one meeting, Rebecca talked about a class that was more challenging. "I actually have to go to class and concentrate," she said, a note of wonder in her voice. This took us into a discussion of whether intelligence is static or if hard mental work can make you "smarter." She believed that you are either smart or you are not, so needing to work hard in a class meant that you were not very bright. I believe that many RFMs share this belief because learning comes so easily. I told her about Dweck's work and that though a certain level of intelligence might be innate, struggling to learn something is necessary and important. For most people, learning requires effort and practice and that the work involved and the resulting success can be most gratifying and can, in fact, be neurologically beneficial.

Because all of her life she found even complex philosophical and mathematical theories easy to understand, Rebecca truly did not realize that her abilities were unusual. I explained how I tell parents of young gifted children to make sure that they find something difficult yet enjoyable for their child to do and require that they stick with it for a specific length of time. At an early age, these experiences will set up a comfort with effort, mistakes, and failure so that the child does not have an unrealistic expectation of learning and intelligence. The child will then take risks with new activities in which they might not excel. Rebecca never had this experience. In fact, her mother boasted about her abilities, so Rebecca felt uncomfortable with her intellect and had no real sense of how to learn something that she did not grasp immediately.

Rebecca was not unusual in the amount of convincing it required to help her see that many of her inner conflicts and self-doubts were largely due to her misunderstanding of her rainforest mind. Her multipotentiality, in particular, had kept her stuck in indecision.

Rebecca wondered if she was in the right field of study. While she loved environmental engineering, she wanted to not only do research, but also implement ideas that would have a real effect on people and the environment. She wanted to change policy and have a greater impact. For her, the academic process felt too slow and the field she was in too narrow, so she was losing interest. She began to research other fields and consider other graduate degrees.

After many weeks of deliberation, Rebecca realized that she had to risk leaving the environmental engineering program and apply to law school. She determined that with a degree in environmental law she could protect the public and the environment, meet her needs to be of service, experience more intellectual challenge and variety, and achieve financial security.

With a sparkle in her eye and relief on her face, I could see that Rebecca was ready to make the change. She understood that her multipotentiality did not have to be a problem. She was not a dilettante or a dabbler. Instead, she was what chemist and novelist Carl Djerassi might call an "intellectual polygamist."[57] She was married to music, philosophy, law, business, environmental policy, and engineering. And she would likely have even more spouses in the future.

Richard: A Spiritual, Inventive Accountant

Richard, 37, a nattily dressed man with a carefully clipped blond beard, had been asked by his wife, Debbie, to seek counseling. During our initial phone conversation, he told me that his marriage was "on the brink of collapse" and that he wanted to do everything he could to save it. His wife had told him that he needed to deal with "anger issues." Even though they had completed some couples counseling, it had not changed all of the problematic dynamics between them.

When we met, Richard told me that he was willing to examine himself, but that he thought Debbie had more of a problem with anger than he did. He admitted, "I might be blind to some aspects of myself," and said that he hoped I might be able to assist. Richard had two young sons and was concerned about their exposure to the tension in the household.

Richard told me he was often anxious and under stress and, as a result, suffered from ulcerative colitis. It seemed important to start with concrete cognitive behavioral work relating to communication skills and stress reduction before looking into deeper reasons for Richard's anxiety.

I learned that Richard worked as a CPA at a large hospital. He was responsible for planning, statistics, and problem-solving around the economics of the organization. It was a stressful job. Given his work, I suspected that he might be more of a linear thinker and less rainforest-minded.

It turned out that Richard had a very creative side. He enjoyed inventing things and was currently working on a new design for a toy. He also had a long-range plan to buy a bookstore and design an adjoining coffee shop. In addition, he had spiritual interests in Zen Buddhism, Hindu singing, and transpersonal counseling. Rather than economics and finance being his sole focus and interest, Richard possessed clear multipotentiality that expanded into both creative and spiritual zones.

It also became apparent that Richard was highly sensitive and had deep emotions, but that he had to shut himself down over the years. He had a hard time identifying and expressing his feelings. So many adult male RFMs I have known were extra-sensitive as children and learned that stereotypical masculinity did not allow for intense emotion and vulnerability.

Because Richard and his wife had started couples counseling again, he did not want to focus on the relationship during our sessions. Instead, he asked to examine his childhood experiences to explore how they might still impact him. In fact, only three years before he started counseling, Richard said that his stepfather had committed suicide. Just ten years before, his mother told him that his stepdad was not his biological father. So these events, in themselves, would be worth exploring.

Additionally, Richard had been identified in second grade as a talented and gifted student, but he chose not to participate. His interests had been in math and science, in particular astrophysics, UFOs, and building machines. He also enjoyed reading Stephen King novels. Once in middle school, he decided to try the gifted program but, when tested again, he did not make the cut. He felt frustrated and confused.

Childhood Replayed

After our initial sessions, Richard told me about some upsetting incidents with his wife. She became quite "angry and unreasonable," breaking and throwing things on occasion. At those times, he would try to reason with her but also found himself losing his temper. He said that there was bipolar disorder in her family, as well as alcoholism and sexual abuse. Debbie was working with a counselor sporadically.

I asked Richard whether the experiences with his wife felt familiar. He told me that the rage reminded him of his father's frequent, angry outbursts and the fights his father had with his mother. He recalled a time when he had to call 911 for the police to come to his home. An only child, Richard hid alone in his room during his parents' fights.

We talked about how childhood experiences are often replayed in adulthood in some form, providing the adult with a chance to change the situation that he was powerless to affect as a child. I described guided imagery and inner child work as a way for him to process his past which might, in turn, improve his relationship. He was immediately willing to try the technique.

We started with a brief guided imagery session that brought surprisingly quick results. Visualizing himself at age five, Richard was able to access sadness and tears that he had long hidden from himself. He felt deep compassion for his child self. Remarkably, within ten minutes, he felt some relief and told me that he even connected with what he called a "nada yoga" sound, which was a part of his spiritual path. He left the session feeling upbeat and, I imagined, hopeful that there was a way to address his concerns.

Over the next few weeks, Richard reported that his relationship with Debbie was improving. She had gained more control of her anger and decided to find a counselor she could see weekly. Richard had also started to implement the active listening technique we had discussed. He was already familiar with the nonviolent communication theory of Marshall Rosenberg, and said he would reread the book he had at home.

As we did more inner child work, Richard continued to feel a loving connection with his child self and build on that connection. In one session, he and his child self worked on building an unusual bike together. This was an activity Richard would have loved doing with his dad and was one of Richard's creative ideas that he did not have time for because of his work schedule and parenting responsibilities. Working on creative projects together with his inner child left Richard feeling more relaxed.

He continued to report progress in his relationship with his wife and said that he would like to meet less often. We started meeting once a month. In one session, Richard wanted to examine his use of alcohol and marijuana. He was worried that he might be tempted to abuse substances, as he liked the feeling of altered consciousness. But feeling that he should work to get there on his own, Richard thought that a greater emphasis on his spiritual practice might help him reduce his substance use.

Seeking Enlightenment

Richard had read a lot of spiritual literature and sincerely wanted to follow a path that would lead toward "enlightenment." But the road looked long and tedious. I suggested he look over the work of Judith Blackstone, especially her book, *Belonging Here: A Guide to the Spiritually Sensitive Person.* Blackstone studied Buddhism and Eastern philosophy and, as a psychotherapist, created a process that included body awareness and psychology that would lead to what she called "fundamental consciousness."

Because Richard had young children and a job that required a lot of energy, he was not able to spend time developing his spirituality or his mulitpotentiality. This led to a sense of frustration. But I suggested that he could at least make time for more pleasure through engaging in his interests in skateboarding and building things, which he could do with his sons, and practicing meditation, even if for just a short amount of time a few days a week.

Richard decided to stop counseling once he felt a more consistent improved relationship with his partner. Debbie agreed that she would be comfortable with him seeing me on an as-need basis. Even though there was more work to do, Richard had made a deeper connection to his emotions and to the playful, creative boy who lived within. He had seen that he could rely on his strong linear cognitive abilities for financial well-being while, at the same time, open to his spiritual songs.

Melanie: My Kids are Gifted, Not Me

Melanie, 38, petite and soft-spoken, originally came to counseling with her husband for a consultation about their oldest son. The boy was highly sensitive and fit the RFM profile, but was not doing well in school. After a few meetings and a couple of check-in sessions over a few years, Melanie decided to see me for her own issues. She said she was depressed and unmotivated, and that, as a mother of three RFMs, she could not keep up with the housework and the kids' needs. She felt enormous guilt. Her children's intensities were overwhelming. She said that her tendency to procrastinate contributed to a pattern of chaos in the family.

At first, we talked about how the RFM traits fit her and not just her children. It took some convincing. We talked about sensitivities and she wrote in an e-mail to me:

> I have changed seats in so many movies, performances, restaurants, classes, etc. because of someone's perfume. Or the way they breathe. I barely passed one of the easiest classes I took in college because I was so distracted by the way the professor mispronounced words. I hate socks, shoes, bras, jewelry, and clothing tags. There are certain colors and combinations of colors that make me [nauseated].

When Melanie started to tell me of all of her interests and abilities, I explained multipotentiality, and she finally agreed that she might be an RFM. Her interests included photography (she had a small business doing portraits), website design (she was doing a couple of volunteer website designs for churches), writing and illustrating children's books (she'd started some sketches), painting, gardening, reading, and generating new ideas about almost anything.

I recommended that Melanie check with her doctor to see whether her low energy and motivation had a physiological basis. They did not. I also suggested she experiment with remedies for sleep and relaxation. Then we began to devote much of our counseling time to helping Melanie find ways to make time for herself and her creativity and to understand that this self-care would be good modeling for her children.

"I've gotten so overwhelmed by the ideas and projects coming into my head that I've tried to convince myself that I could just turn them off and just be happy being a mom," Melanie told me. "The thought of ignoring all my ideas was even more depressing than trying to keep up with them, so I abandoned the plan. Sometimes, there are so many things that I want to do, it's paralyzing and I end up doing nothing."

Because we'd spent time talking about her gifted children in earlier meetings, Melanie was familiar with much of the information I was now asking her to apply to herself. We did not have to meet too many times before she put the pieces together. Because her childhood family seemed pretty functional, our work stayed focused on the understanding of her RFM and her multipotentiality. She said, "I was frustrated the other day because I could not think of one thing I could do fulltime and be content with it. But then I remembered that I don't have to limit myself to one thing and it's not necessarily a character flaw."

At our last session, Melanie said she had noticed much progress. She felt less guilt and fear around not being a perfect mom and was taking time to nurture her arts interests. I have worked with many women who tirelessly support their RFM children but do not recognize their own abilities. They feel a strong sense of responsibility and deep love for their children but, at the same time, are embarrassed and even ashamed by feelings of frustration with the mundane tasks or boredom at the lack of intellectual stimulation.

Melanie felt a great sense of relief being able to talk about this openly. Just hearing that she was not alone renewed her energy. She said, "The other day, I had a friend comment to me that she was trying to be supermom this week and it wasn't working. I told her not to feel bad because I was just shooting for mediocre and I wasn't even hitting that."

She admitted that though she felt somewhat overwhelmed with her family's upcoming move to another city due to her husband's new job, she felt more confident in her ability to handle it all.

Several months later, I heard from Melanie. She said she had been pleasantly surprised at how well her children had adjusted to the move and their new schools. She was feeling greater strength and optimism and looking forward to continuing to develop her interests in photography, web design, and writing children's books. She said that when she was not "scheduling and taxiing three kids around," she had a part-time job in the school office, joined a book club and a soccer team, started teaching herself to play the ukulele, did "fun artsy projects around the house," and was growing flowers and vegetables in her greenhouse.

In addition to being a mother of gifted children, she also had her own rainforest mind. And she was ready to use it.

Strategies

❧ When choosing careers, know your values. Craft a career that combines many of your interests. Choose something(s) which you are passionate about, that gives you a sense of purpose, and that will meet your need to make a difference. Consider self-employment. Know that you can change jobs and careers. Grieve over the choices that you do not take. Use TED.com to find out what others are doing. Think BIG.

❧ Spend time at puttylike.com. Join the community of multipotentialites.

❧ Think out of the box. Consider becoming a consultant and speaker in an area which combines many of your interests or a researcher/ journalist/intern for an organization like NPR. Read up on Ira Glass to find out how he started *This American Life* or Ira Flatow of *Science Friday*, both popular, intellectually-appealing radio programs. Look into starting your own podcasts.

❧ Read *The Renaissance Soul*, by Margaret Lobenstine. There are many excellent concrete exercises in the book that can help you figure out how to manage and manifest your careers.

❧ Take advantage of career centers at community colleges and universities. Take online tests to find out more about how your interests can combine into a career. Staff members are often well-trained and can suggest resources or directions you might not think of on your own.

❧ *Be a Free Range Human*, by Marianne Cantwell, is an excellent guide to creating career paths.

- Keep a special journal devoted to your ideas for projects/careers. Use it to write, draw, mind-map, list, or plan without any attention to practicality or reality. These may never be developed, which is fine. This idea comes from *Refuse to Choose*, by Barbara Sher (barbarasher.com). Her book is full of support and understanding along with strategies and tools for creating a satisfying set of careers. She offers some interesting classes and workshops on this topic and describes her own dance with multipotentiality.

- Explore Martha Beck's writing at marthabeck.com, as well as other life coaches who have creative ideas.

- Amy Cuddy's book, *Presence*, will help you build your confidence in difficult situations using simple techniques.

- If you are a parent, appreciate the complexity, responsibility, and awesomeness of your choice to raise a precious human being. Notice how parenting allows you to use many of your abilities and tap into some of your interests. At the same time, give yourself permission to experience conflicting feelings when you feel overwhelmed, frustrated, or intellectually under-stimulated. Know that you will make mistakes and that admitting them will allow your children to feel that they can be less than perfect.

- If you are raising a child like you, read *Raising Your Spirited Child*, by Mary Kurcinka. Listen to what your child is saying and feeling—and also to what s/he is not saying. Try to control your urge to fix, advise, and direct. At the same time, it is important that you set limits, are consistent, maintain healthy boundaries, and learn how to avoid power struggles. Help your child appreciate deep emotion, but also find ways to contain and channel passionate expression. Another good parenting resource is Charlotte Reznick at imageryforkids.com.

ॐ If you love research, writing, and speaking about science topics, check out the writer Mary Roach's books and consider a similar career path.

ॐ If you are in a job that meets your needs for predictability or financial stability, but you want to change some of the ways things are done in the company, read the book *Rebels at Work*, by Carmen Medina and Lois Kelly. Medina and Kelly have created a detailed guide on how to carefully and conscientiously make a difference within a complex system.

ॐ Explore empoweryou.com and books by Laurence Boldt on finding career paths.

ॐ Give yourself a break if you have difficulty making decisions. Understand that your divergent thinking, your openness to new ideas and your love of research may contribute to this "problem." Explain it to the important people in your life so that they have more patience with you.

ॐ Noks Nauta, a physician in the Netherlands, has conducted research about gifted adults and work. Find her articles at noksnauta.nl/english.html.

ॐ Remind yourself that there are times when decisions need to be made quickly and that if you do not like the results, you can often revise or rework the outcome later. Work on your perfectionism, if that is part of what is going on. Remember that you can produce high quality without perfection; that if you end up making the wrong decision, it is not usually a tragedy, and that some remarkable inventions came from "wrong" decisions. Bad decisions can make great keynote speeches and humorous books.

Chapter Five

Going It Alone

Many parents dream of having accomplished children, but children who manifest genius at a young age may prove utterly confounding. They are likely to suffer from asynchrony: having an intellectual age at odds with their emotional age. As a result, with no real peers, such children may be desperately lonely.

~Andrew Solomon[58]

Out of Sync

Loneliness may be the number one challenge for the RFM. And it often starts early.

You are six years old and not invited to birthday parties. Or you are invited, but have to leave early because you cannot stand the noise. You are eight and join the soccer team because your parents want you to be "normal," but you would rather lie on the field watching the clouds than run after a ball. Or you are fourteen and prefer Jane Austen to Justin Bieber.

Understandably, it is hard to find peers—kids who share your complexities, interests, and sensitivities. The other six-year-olds did not want to talk about the BBC documentaries you saw or your family vacation to NASA. Or maybe you were like Thelma Golden, the chief curator of the Studio Museum of Harlem, who said, "The Museum of Modern Art was my Disney World."[59]

In school, because you were placed with your same-aged peers, you may have felt that you lacked social skills. In fact, your ability to communicate was just fine when you were with older children who matched your mental age or when you were speaking with adults,[60] but the children in your classroom thought you were a weirdo or a nerd and ignored you on the playground. The rejection was painful; the memories still sting.

Interestingly, you probably did not connect the rejection to your intellect. Like my 32-year-old client, Elizabeth, who would think to herself, "You can't possibly *not* understand what I'm talking about. This is so easy," you assumed that what you could do was not extraordinary. Anyone could do it if they tried. Instead, you blamed yourself for your clumsy communication skills.

Another factor that may have contributed to your loneliness was your uneven development, or asynchrony. You may have had advanced mental abilities in some areas and not in others. Or you may have been unable to put thoughts into action at the level that you envisioned them.[61] For example, while you may have been playing chess with adults or reading Shakespeare at age nine, your math skills may have been average or your athletic abilities may have been negligible. Maybe you tried to grasp infinity at age eight but were stumped by long division. Perhaps you could deeply appreciate music theory but not yet play your instrument as well as you desired because your body needed more time to mature. Or, you may have been devastated by your inability to draw like the artists you so admired.

Often, your mind will grasp the concept but your body will be unable to execute it. You become frustrated because you cannot produce what you envision. It would be hard to feel like you belonged with, say, the other eight- and nine-year-old kids who were much more in tune with each other. Your struggles were different from theirs and they may have rejected you for it.

Asynchrony, then, is another phenomenon that sets you apart and alone. Most children do not have such glaring differences in their developmental levels. They are clearer about where they fit. You are lonely because you do not fit in any one place.

Even now, you may find that the conversations are not deep enough or fast enough, or no one quite gets your sense of humor. You may be the one everyone comes to for advice, but when you need a confidant, no one's home. Or, as one client reported, you may be playing Scrabble on your iPhone with people around the world and they all drop out of the game when you play without holding back.

Navigating the Workplace

In a work setting, you might find that you are resented for your creative ideas, or that you become irritated and impatient as you wait for your colleagues to draw the conclusions you made hours before. Your standards for quality and morality and your idealism may not match that of your coworkers or supervisors.[62] Office politics may bore you and, even though you enjoy a hearty collaboration, you may not be a skillful team player.[63]

Another challenge at the workplace might be the speed at which you get things done. My energetic client, Roberta, spoke of feeling like a "slacker" because at times she had nothing to do at her job. And yet she accomplished everything required and then some, much faster than her predecessor. Roberta felt awkward with her co-workers, who seemed put off by her exceptional skills and speed. Her supervisor was threatened by her questions and competence. Roberta would have loved collaborations or socializing with colleagues after work, but they were not interested.

Bruce, a young father, said that he was either idealized or demonized in his job designing computer games. There was no middle ground. He described his high expectations and desire to move as fast as he could. When he could see the "whole picture" or intuitively know how to proceed on a project, he would be frustrated by co-workers who did not share his vision and who resented him for "patronizing" them. He wanted to speed down the open highway but was constantly running into roadblocks. He compared himself to the lonely boy in the film *Rushmore* who was in prep school answering the calculus questions no one else could, organizing after-school clubs, experimenting with bizarre notions, and being rejected and ridiculed by the other students.

As my client Melinda reflected

Why don't others enjoy documentaries, museums, and history the way I do? I am already stressed out and saddened that I won't be able to read every book ever written, speak every language spoken, or travel to every country in my lifetime. Not one person I have ever known feels the same way about learning and absorbing— transcending really. Who cares about skinny jeans? My thinking cap is always tied tight but my [gas]tank is always half empty.

In her article, "Discovering the Gifted Ex-Child," Stephanie Tolan wrote:

A gifted adult may find herself in the workplace and/ or outside associating with many individuals who do not share the complexity and depth of her perceptions. . . . She may have to weigh her words, simplify her conceptions, hold herself back in conversation. This experience is both tiring and frustrating. Particularly if she does not understand or accept her giftedness, she (and others) may interpret her difficulty as social ineptitude.[64]

Being faster, more thorough, or more ethical than your colleagues can result in a sense of isolation. You want to belong and have coworkers with whom you can share your ideas. Instead, you may be ignored, disliked, or even scapegoated.

Containing your Enthusiasm

If you have a strong verbal ability, you may love discussion and debate and have a hard time containing your enthusiasm for the many topics that interest you. As Mary-Elaine Jacobsen puts it, you may "love to play with speech patterns, twists of a phrase, and hidden meanings, or simply enjoy the sound of certain words as they roll off the tongue."[65] And you may be aching to find someone who matches your fast wit or who can follow you when you leap through ideas and jump to creative theories or unusual speculations. Individuals who run at normal speed may not grasp the depth of your deep frustration, as you race on ahead, alone.

My client, Veronica, described herself as a "high content" individual. Like Veronica, you have multitudes of thoughts, theories, perceptions, and stories that you want to share (especially if you are an extrovert). Unfortunately, you find that many people either cannot follow what you are saying or quickly lose interest. Other times, you need to provide so much background, backstory, and context that you get discouraged and deflated.

Because of your quest for knowledge and, perhaps, to escape from an overwhelming world and rejection from peers, you are likely an avid reader. Books may have meant everything to you when you were younger. They may still. "People will always let you down at some point if you let them. Books are some of my best friends, best vacations, and best childhood memories," wrote one of my clients.

When you were a child, you may have had to insist to librarians that you were, in fact, old enough to read Toni Morrison or Alice Walker. Shonda Rhimes, a writer and TV producer, said she was reading *The French Lieutenant's Woman* when she was eight and that the freedom to read was vital in setting the groundwork for her future. Writer Amy Tan recalled, "It was almost sinful how much I liked it."[66]

Many people may make the assumption that you have no needs or that you are "so smart" that you will figure it out yourself. And, in fact, you often do prefer your own ideas because when you have asked for help, it is often inadequate. The juxtaposition is quite a bind—one that you really cannot explain to other folks without feeling weird, guilty, arrogant, or frustrated.

Intimate Partnerships

You may be challenged in partnerships, too. Where do you find someone who loves your eccentricities, curiosities, and passions and who also wants to live with you and them forever after? Better yet, where do you find someone who shares some of your eccentricities, curiosities, and passions and who you still want to live with? Ellen Fiedler, author and consultant in gifted education, states:

> *Gifted adults may have to search far and wide to find others who share their sometimes esoteric interests or even to find someone who laughs at their sometimes quirky jokes. . . . If connections that lead to intimacy are not successful, or when attempts to form close relationships explode in their faces, isolation is typically the result, with some gifted young adults distancing themselves from others, more convinced than ever that they are aliens from another planet and that there is no one here on earth with whom they can relate.*[67]

Like everything else about you, it is complicated. If you do find someone with whom you "fit," how does an intimate relationship work between two highly intense, sensitive, and ruminating individuals? Would it be like winning the lottery? Landing on Mars? Too many cans of Mountain Dew? Yes.

You can be sure it will be, at the very least, dynamic and exciting in its own particularly intense way. And, as in all intimate relationships, your issues will arise, your buttons will be pushed, and both of your hearts will be expanded, contracted, and repaired. It could get you into therapy. And that might be good. The relationship could astonish you. You might discover layers of yourself that have been buried for a long time.

If there's no person available, what about finding companionship in your religion or your spirituality or in nature? According to author Steven Pressfield, if you are following your true path and tapping into your muse, then you will not be alone because a whole team of spiritual allies or angels—whatever you call them—will be at your side.[68] I suspect that the company of allies and angels might be frustrating for the extroverts among you who need real, flesh-and-blood people to feed your appetite for interaction. And yet, it might be comforting to know that, in a spiritual sense, you are not really alone. And, I'm guessing that some of you might find deep satisfaction by simply gazing at the night sky.

Years ago, I watched a quirky TV program called *Ally McBeal*. In one episode, her wacky therapist advised her to find her "Pips," as in Gladys Knight and the Pips. She explained that everyone has a team of back-up singers who provide needed harmonies and help you get through life's rough times. So, if all else fails and no one answers when you call, find your Pips and start singing.

Whitney: Rebellious Bibliophile

Thirty-year-old Whitney was a graduate student in anthropology and women's studies. She came to counseling because she said, "I reached the end of my own abilities to fix myself." Whitney's mother had died a year earlier and her intimate relationship was "faltering." In describing her goals in counseling, she wrote, "I want to stop carrying the weight of my family's legacy, to untangle the mess in my head, to be free." Whitney had a history of difficult relationships with partners and trouble finding emotionally healthy friends.

She described a bipolar, physically and sexually abusive mother. Her father was kind and loving to her but didn't stand up to stop the abuse. Both parents were intellectually gifted but, according to Whitney, were "spectacularly unsuccessful in the real world." When Whitney was twenty-two her father died suddenly.

As a child in school, Whitney was bullied. She was excited about learning and a talkative extravert who teachers dismissed with impatience and children rejected. It appeared that Whitney was at the higher end of the gifted continuum.

As with most of my clients, we worked on two main tracks. Track one was the long road to healing from severe childhood trauma. Convincing Whitney through lots of counseling processes that the abuse was not her fault, that she was, in fact, worthy of love, was the more complicated task. When children are abused day in and day out, they are programmed to believe that they are worthless. Over time, in a deeply supportive counseling relationship, clients can start to accept and love themselves. Whitney gradually felt more trust in me and allowed herself to grieve the losses she experienced for so many years. Because her memories had created symptoms of post-traumatic stress, we used techniques, such as EMDR, that had a body-centered component.

Childhood abuse has an enormous impact on all aspects of the person. Whitney, like many gifted folks, had shown a powerful resilience. In spite of her rejecting, critical, abusing mother, Whitney was a kind, loving, competent woman. The damage was evident, though, in her distorted view of herself and her inability to believe she was worthy of love. It took time for her to feel safe enough in therapy to allow herself to cry, to trust.

Whitney also did much self-examination. She particularly enjoyed art projects and used journaling and other art forms to delve deeper. She worked on communicating with partners and friends to set up better boundaries and improve her relationships. She was a big reader, always looking for resources that would expand her knowledge, particularly in the areas of body image and women's issues.

The other track was simpler but also quite necessary. Even though Whitney had experienced academic success, she didn't identify as gifted or understand the traits. She wrote about this: "There were—and still are—so many times in my life I felt an unbridgeable distance between myself and others, like I fundamentally see the world in a different way that I can't even explain because we don't speak the same language." Even though Whitney found friends, she felt lonely much of the time. She was often the caretaker in the relationship, giving love and support but not getting much back.

She wrote:

I get hungry for people who are socially competent and intellectual and curious about literally everything and creative and broad-minded and motivated by justice . . . People who care and feel deeply but also think in complex wide-ranging ways.

With partners, Whitney found individuals who were generally intelligent, possibly gifted, but emotionally abusive. This is common when one has grown up abused. Even though she was an optimist, Whitney felt despair over finding a truly loving and kind, intimate relationship. And with both friends and partners, Whitney had difficulty setting boundaries and asking for what she needed. Being gifted, this was even more challenging because it wasn't easy finding other sensitive souls.

As time passed in our work together, Whitney graduated with her master's degree. Her advisor may have been the first teacher who recognized and appreciated her giftedness, telling her she was the brightest student she had ever worked with. Whitney and I continued therapy as she looked for employment. Fairly quickly she found a job that was not in her field of study but suited her well: social services.

Whitney was a case manager and wildly successful with clients. The combination of her sensitivity, empathy, energy, and intelligence worked well with the population of families she helped. She often took on extra responsibilities to keep herself busy. In meetings, she saw the big picture and solutions long before her colleagues. So, she was restless in the job when she had accomplished her goals and was not recognized for her skills, typical frustrations of RFMs on the job. It was likely that Whitney would find more challenging, financially rewarding work as her confidence grew but this position was satisfying her need to make a difference.

Over our years together, Whitney made enormous progress. She could acknowledge how severe her losses had been and grow more and more self-accepting. Her self-criticism decreased significantly. She began to recognize her many strengths and imagine that she would indeed find deep friendships and a kind loving partner.

Whitney described her experience this way:

> *I keep hoping to meet people with whom I can relax and be just me, all of me, unafraid to let them see who I really am, in all my dorky, questing, art-loving, social justice obsessed, bibliophile, rebellious, intersectional feminist, world-changing glory.*

Ruth: Bridging Distances

Fifty-two-year-old Ruth initially came to see me for help with her teenage son. He had been identified as gifted in preschool and needed assistance navigating the school system. As we talked, she found that many of the characteristics linked with giftedness also applied to her, though she observed, "I don't really see myself as above average." But her years of loneliness and anxiety started to make sense when put in this context. She wanted to find out more.

Ruth described early experiences of being different: an avid reader who loved thinking and analyzing more than playing with Barbies. She was a seven-year-old worrier about world peace who was rarely invited to birthday parties.

School held painful memories. In second grade, she recalled completing an entire reading workbook in one evening and proudly showing her teacher the next day. Her teacher reprimanded her for "working ahead" and had her sit in her seat and color in the pictures on the workbook pages while the other students caught up to her. Ruth had entered school with eager anticipation, but this type of experience happened repeatedly and gradually dampened her enthusiasm for school. She explained, "I learned quickly not to draw attention to myself by answering questions or being too enthusiastic about the subjects the teacher was presenting."

Ruth was self-employed as a policy analyst in the renewable energy field. This career met her needs for freedom to work at her own pace with lots of variety and contacts around the world. Her work also allowed her to contribute to the betterment of society and explore her many interests. She was grateful to have found a meaningful niche.

Yet, Ruth had difficulty finding friends. There was an intensity about her and a speed in her thinking and speech that many other people found uncomfortable. She also felt a strong need to examine issues deeply; she was not very interested in small talk.

I am definitely a fast thinker and this has become more apparent to me over the years. I get frustrated when I have to stop and explain things to people that seem very obvious to me. Being able to think at my own pace is such a relief. Finding someone who enjoys exploring a topic at that pace is exhilarating.

She did have a few friends: one in Sweden, one in Malaysia, and one in Minnesota. Technology helped her stay in touch, but was not the same as in-person contact.

There was also tension in Ruth's partnership. She had married a man eight years her junior when she was in her mid-30s. She described him as sensitive, well-read, and bright, but she was often frustrated by differences in style, complexity, and depth. For example, even though Ruth worked full-time, she still ran the household, handling finances, domestic chores, and other responsibilities. When her home was being remodeled, she was the contractor in charge. She was the more active parent, monitoring their son's schoolwork and attending school events.

Not surprisingly, her husband Robert felt intimidated and insecure around her and had difficulty communicating his discomfort or any of his feelings. He was overwhelmed by the intensity of her speech, emotion, and energy. Unfortunately, he also had trouble focusing on and completing tasks and had a difficult time making decisions.

Because Ruth did not realize there was a basic difference in their capacity for achievement, she assumed that Robert was lazy and choosing not to keep up with her. This misunderstanding created tension between them and more loneliness for Ruth. Because she was extremely high functioning, Robert looked fairly ineffectual even though he was bright, perceptive, and caring. I suggested that Ruth try couples counseling with a therapist I knew who understood giftedness. Robert agreed to go.

During their couples work, it became apparent that Robert was also likely on the gifted spectrum, but introverted and less multi-dimensional. Ruth suggested that he might have ADHD, which would account for his difficulty with follow-through and decisions, and he agreed to see a practitioner for an evaluation.

Ruth reported that her relationship with her husband improved markedly after they both could acknowledge and appreciate their similarities as well as their differences. She said, "We attend lectures and classes and enjoy doing research on natural history systems that we encounter on our long hikes . . . we can each be as geeky as we want."

The new understanding of her rainforest mind also helped her in her quest for friendship. Knowing what qualities to look for, she began to use her intuition to identify like-minded souls and get to know them. Ruth's loneliness eased as she made new friends and better understood her partner, as she owned the right to stop hiding "the vibrant life inside" and be herself in all of her rainforest radiance.

Strategies

❧ When looking for friends, do things you love and keep your eyes open for other RFMs. Now that you know what to look for, get out there! It is likely fellow RFMs will be shy or awkward for the same reasons that you are, so be brave and take the first step. Start a conversation, suggest going for a walk or out for coffee. Use your commonality as a place to start talking. The person is likely to be grateful that you took the risk. If you are out of practice, you might start by finding friends for specific activities, rather than looking for the one friend who has everything. You may go to films with one person, discuss books with another, and do tai chi with a third.

❧ Let go of the idea that your friends all need to be about your age.

❧ When people compliment you or overreact to your accomplishments, simply smile and say thank you.

❧ Look online for seminars, summer programs at universities, think tank opportunities, conferences, travel options, contests, mentorships, and internships in one of your fields of interest. Stay in touch with the people you meet there.

❧ For extroverts, loneliness can be particularly difficult. If you do not have a partner or a roommate to help you feel less alone at home, go to a coffee shop with WiFi and bring your laptop so you can write and answer e-mails, read, and work on projects. You may feel comforted by the sounds of the other people even if you are not directly interacting with them. If you become a regular, it may feel good to see familiar faces of the staff and other regular customers and maybe even get to know some of them.

❧ If you're an introvert, join Susan Cain's community at quietrev.com. Susan Cain is the author of *Quiet: The Power of Introverts in a World that Can't Stop Talking.*

❧ If you have trouble making small talk and you are in a situation where it is required, start by asking questions about the other person. People usually enjoy talking about themselves.

❧ Make a list of people you admire: writers, artists, philosophers, saints, skeptics, and scientists. They do not need to be living and they do not need to be people you have actually met. When you feel lonely, write a letter to one of these folks expressing your feelings, thoughts, and questions. Then, write the letter that they would write back to you.

❧ Remember that what is obvious to you may not be so to others.

❧ Do not believe what you hear about how you will never find a partner because there are not enough single folks, or you are too intense and critical to be satisfied, or there is something inherently wrong with you. First, decide whether you even want a partner. If you are not sure, or if you feel some invisible barrier, do some writing about it and see where that leads. You will want to explore your fears by talking to them and listening closely. Your fears may give you valuable information. You can work productively with those insights, either in therapy or your journal.

❧ When you feel that your fears about partnership are more or less calmed and contained (this could take a while), use an art form you enjoy to "connect with" your future partner before s/he arrives.

❧ Use your sensitivity to the natural world to find comfort and friendship with trees, birds, and the land where you live.

❧ If you are already in a partnership and want some guidance, I recommend books by Susan Johnson, John Gottman, John Welwood, and Esther Perel. If you want to get deeply analytical, try books by Harville Hendrix. I recommend couples counseling, too, with someone who understands giftedness, or at least is willing to read some articles you provide, or who is likely gifted him/herself. You can be sure that any unresolved childhood issues will come up, so you may also want to consider individual therapy. Even if only one of you is willing to do therapy, a lot of shifting can happen for both of you. If your partner is not an RFM, you might need to develop some ways to accommodate different levels of awareness and intensity. If, for example, you communicate like a fire hose, your partner may need to ask for the garden hose version of you when s/he gets overwhelmed.

❧ Learn the Argentine tango. The tango is a difficult dance to learn and requires intensity, sensitivity, creativity, intuition, and persistence—a perfect dance for and a great way to meet other RFMs. If you learn how to lead the Argentine tango, you will get to experience being followed in a way that does not happen easily during conversations about, say, string theory.

Chapter Six

School Daze

"Waiting" was the most common response when Tracy Cross of the College of William and Mary asked thirteen thousand kids in seven states to describe in one word their experience as gifted children. "They said they were always waiting for teachers to move ahead, waiting for classmates to catch up, waiting to learn something new—always waiting."

~Tom Clynes[69]

A Former Insider

As I mentioned in the introduction, I started my career as a sixth grade teacher in a junior high school. I taught science, language arts, and social studies. I have fond memories of those days and can recall my enthusiasm with students and my willingness, along with many of my colleagues, to spend unpaid hours outside of the classroom correcting papers and planning lessons. In short, I feel that I can speak about schooling as a former insider. And for RFMs, the picture is less than ideal.

First, you may not realize that some RFMs do not do well in school. In fact, your schooling experiences could have been a source of great pain and confusion.[70] It is assumed that the brightest kids are the ones who get good grades in school, do their homework, follow the rules, and achieve. Not necessarily. Mary-Elaine Jacobsen agrees, "[S]traight-A report cards and scholarships to Julliard are often missing from the backgrounds of even the most intelligent adults."[71]

Brenda, a client with three young children, described her experience this way:

> *I would hear over and over again that I had potential but I just didn't work hard enough. That wasn't true. I've always loved learning new things and exploring new concepts. I would read through my textbooks excited with the prospect of learning something new, even before school started. It was when classes began that I got bored and frustrated. Things went too slowly, and often I felt that teachers ignored what I said or wrote me off. And I'd always end up with teachers who would take it upon themselves to fix my slacker ways, using tough love and meanness as a substitute for real human connection and understanding.*

Starving for Stimulation

The frustrating thing is that, like Brenda, you probably love learning and are starving for intellectual stimulation. Eileen, one of my teenage clients, described herself as "ravenous" when it came to learning new things. You may have been an early reader and eager to start school. But by third grade, or perhaps by the third day of kindergarten, you became seriously disappointed. And it is possible that you blamed yourself for not fitting in or for not being normal when the problem lay with underfunded schools, students not receiving adequate support for their unique gifts and interests, or teachers pressured to raise test scores rather than innovate and get to know their students deeply.

John, in his 60s when he came to see me, said he remembered reading *Thirty Seconds Over Tokyo* in third grade. His teacher discovered the book and insisted that, from then on, he get her permission before he checked out any library books. Children taunted him with "you think you're so smart." He did not think he was so smart.

Perhaps some teachers did not recognize your intelligence because of your sensitivity or your cultural need to put the group first or because your first language was not English. If they did see that you were smart, they may not have known how to meet your academic needs. Maybe some even felt threatened by all of your questions, your creative thinking, and your intense desire to know.[72] Perhaps they were simply annoyed by your need to correct their spelling errors.

In *The I of the Beholder*, Annemarie Roeper writes,

> *Many gifted children had, and still do have, a most difficult time all during their school careers because they simply did not fit in. These difficulties are expressed in many different ways, such as an inability to concentrate on homework or sit still in boring classes.*

She goes on, "Albert Einstein attended school sporadically, but ultimately, he felt that a lack of schooling was the best thing that happened to him. It allowed him to be free to pursue his own inner agenda."[73]

Sometimes, teachers simply misunderstand who a student is and what she needs. When you were dying to learn about fractals but could not for the life of you remember multiplication facts, or when you kept losing your homework even though you knew you put it in your backpack, or when you did not finish assignments because they did not measure up to your standards, you may have been told you were lazy, not working up to your potential. But they did not know that you'd read *Huckleberry Finn* three years ago or that you understood the concept of photosynthesis the first time around. They did not know that in your daydreams you were designing new worlds on other planets, creating new languages and cultures, and that your inner world was way more fascinating than life in Room 10.

Emilie Graslie's inner world was a fine example of this. I came across her blog after hearing about her on NPR. She created the educational program on YouTube called *The Brain Scoop* that is now based at The Field Museum in Chicago, the largest natural history museum in the world. Her job title is Chief Curiosity Correspondent. This is what she said about school:

> *I hated high school, and I was pretty vocal about my distaste. I was what the teachers referred to as "disruptive." I hardly ever followed the rules, made exceptions for myself at every opportunity, skipped class, cried in the bathroom at lunchtime, and despised who I was. When I told the school counselor that I didn't know what I wanted to do after graduation, or that I wasn't even sure if I wanted to go to college, she recommended the military because it was a disciplined environment. I wasn't violent, I was just . . . vocal. Outspoken. Upset. Frustrated.*[74]

In a striking example of how much faster a gifted child can learn concepts and just how many classroom hours might be wasted, writer and educator Marylou Streznewski cites a study of mathematically precocious eighth graders who take "between three and fifteen hours to learn first-year algebra well enough to achieve a good grade on a standardized exam. Most of them are required to sit through 150 hours of classroom instruction to accomplish the same thing."[75]

No one told you that the system was inadequate, so you probably thought that you were. Writer Diane Ackerman described her schooling experiences this way:

> *This creative hunger has not always been a boon. For many years, it alienated me from family and playmates, who found my mental fantasia odd. In kindergarten I was reprimanded for using too many colors to draw a tree's thick chewy-looking bark. As a college freshman, I flunked Logic.*[76]

And perhaps you were the kid who kept trying in spite of it all. You did the homework, paid close attention in class, and scored well on tests. What was your reward? You were the "teacher's pet" or the "nerd," rejected by other kids because of your passions for words, nature, galaxies, numbers, and big ideas, and because you just did not understand why hanging out at the mall was so cool.

No Time for Amazement

Some of you found your niche at a good university. But others of you either did not go to college or, if you did, just found more of the same. Mario Molina, who won the Nobel Prize in chemistry, said that he benefited most in college when he was given permission to explore beyond the typical boundaries and that he learned best at his own pace out of the classroom.[77] Even in college, then, you may have been waiting for your peers to catch up. Or, perhaps you were not allowed to design an interdisciplinary program because you were supposed to pick one narrow area of study.

Or maybe you had an experience like my marine biologist client, Ray, in his mycology and algae class. The professor appreciated his drawings but told him to "pick up the pace." Ray told me, "I was too enraptured by the amazing organisms I was watching under my microscope. I got in trouble for taking the time to be amazed."

By the way, Ray, in his rainforest-mindedness, ran into trouble way before college. He tried to avoid elementary school with multiple stomachaches, was placed in a special education classroom in high school, and took fifteen years to get his undergraduate degree.

My client Denise said, "I spent hours doing things I already understood. I came out as an adult with an almost panic reaction to the prospect of boredom. There's grief about what I could have learned, how I could have grown my brain if I'd been challenged."

Even so, a few teachers along the way inspired Ray and Denise and I am betting that a teacher or two inspired you, loved teaching your inquisitive mind. In fact, Denise added, "My sixth grade teacher saw me spending most of my time reading behind my desk. She slipped me *Fellowship of the Ring* one day and smiled saying, 'I think you might like this.' I loved it."

There are teachers we remember for life because they influenced us to become a NASA scientist or a poet or they believed in us when no one else did. Maybe they gave us a book to read that changed everything. Teaching is challenging, especially now that many classrooms are crowded and children have a large range of abilities and needs. But it is sad and deeply frustrating—OK, appalling—to see how poorly designed our education system is for the RFM.

If you spent years in school frustrated, despairing, and lonely, now you know why. Equal education is not all students in a class doing the same thing at the same time. Equality in education means all students get their individual academic needs met, including you.[78]

Tom: Too Much Zeal

Tom, 55, was the son of immigrant parents from South America. He expressed a desire to be "happy" or "at least content." He wanted to learn better communication skills for his personal and professional relationships. His goals were to gain self-awareness and have an opportunity "to speak out loud to a third party" rather than endlessly "ruminate" in his head. Tearing up, he then said that his father-in-law, with whom he was quite close, had died about five months prior to our meeting.

Tom did not think of himself as gifted since he had done poorly in school and had not completed a college degree. He said that even though he was passionate about learning, he experienced high levels of anxiety during tests and that he had been in college for many years but never finished.

Tom suspected that his years in a Catholic school contributed to his anxiety in academic settings. He described memories of physical abuse by nuns for small infractions. He was bullied by the other children. Tom recalled having particular difficulty memorizing multiplication facts. He still did not know them but, "isn't that what calculators are for?" he said with a grin.

I asked him to describe his experiences in school and he said:

I learned how to swear there. I learned to avoid getting caught by the bigger kids and the nuns. I was the second-fastest runner in my class and I made use of the speed. So did my mouth, which sometimes got me into trouble that my feet couldn't get me out of. I learned when to risk getting the [expletive] kicked out of me and when not to.

Even when Tom went to a public junior high, the situation did not improve. The curriculum was not challenging and his peers were unkind. Tom's parents became more proactive in high school and found a math tutor for him. Describing the tutor he explained:

She gave me the tools to interpret the language of mathematics. I chose it as an area of interest because of her. I excelled in mathematics for some time after that. It was as though she imbued a mathematical confidence in me that served other aspects of my life.

Suddenly, mathematics was fascinating; so much so that he majored in the field in college and has since become quite successful as an IT expert.

I told Tom how often I hear parents talk about their bright children struggling with basic skills such as multiplication, spelling, and handwriting, while excelling in complex subjects such as philosophy and calculus, and how this discrepancy confuses them and their children's teachers. Tom said that he still felt ill and anxious when faced with examinations; in fact, he was trying to decide whether to study for a set of computer credentialing tests that he had failed some years back.

Tom's anxiety around tests was excessive, so I wanted to explore it a bit more. In talking of his years in college, it became apparent that he felt tremendous pressure to succeed, but that his early associations with academic struggles made success difficult. He also noted that he would get exhausted after even a short stint of reading.

Only after dropping out of college did he discover that he needed glasses and that a portion of his trouble in school was likely due to vision problems. He said that leaving college for the last time was "the hardest thing I ever did." I could see that my task was to help Tom recognize that circumstances, not intelligence, were at the root of his missing college degree.

Not Bad for a Dropout

Clearly, Tom loved solving problems, deriving deep pleasure from diving into complicated computer hardware, software, or networking issues. He related to many other RFM characteristics. He said he was highly sensitive and had trouble hiding his emotions and that this expressiveness had made relationships difficult. He was concerned that because of this sensitivity, counseling might be "opening a can of worms." I reassured Tom that his emotions were welcome and that we could look at ways to move slowly.

Tom also mentioned that he had been accused of having too much "zeal." He had been told he needed to "grow up" and become a more restrained adult. We talked about the pressure on men to hide their sensitivities, empathy, and sadness. I have known many gifted men who were ridiculed as children and, as a result, repressed their range of emotion. Tom was among them.

One of his goals was to improve his marriage by finding better ways to communicate with his wife, Jayne. He ran his computer business out of his home and Jayne managed the website, bookkeeping, and all of the office details. Not surprisingly, they ran into difficulty because there were not any natural boundaries around the work time or space, and the nature of the job required that Tom work odd hours and weekends. That arrangement would be challenging for anyone and it sounded as though Tom and Jayne handled it fairly well. But there was tension between them. We talked about ways Tom could improve his listening skills so that he could allow Jayne to talk and not feel as though he needed to fix things or offer solutions. I told him that, in general, women want to share feelings without problem-solving per se and that being listened to was, in fact, the solution.

Tom began to practice active listening with Jayne and reported some success. He also decided to carve out a regular evening once a week for a date night, no matter what else might be brewing with work. Both ideas relieved some of the tension. Tom also needed to feel heard and understood by me so that he could release work and relationship pressures in our sessions and allow his grief to surface over his father-in-law's death.

Tom said that a point of contention with his wife was the amount of time he spent giving his computer knowledge away to friends and relatives. He explained that he was concerned about the harm the electronics industry was causing to the environment and to people in China and other countries who labored to build the gadgets we use here and discard so quickly. He figured that the more he fixed people's devices, the longer they would keep them and the less waste would be generated. He also financially supported a local electronics/computer recycler and actively encouraged his customers to recycle their phones, computers, and other such items.

Then, in one session, Tom told me how he started in the IT world. He had taught himself years ago by "playing with the machines" and reading the "twenty-pound book" that explained how it all worked. Not bad for a college dropout.

Life in the Jungle

Tom and I talked about his family and he told me that his four siblings and both of his parents had college degrees. Somehow, they had managed to navigate the system where he had not. For years, he interpreted that to mean that he was just not so bright. But, in a moment of reflection, he paused and then said, "I was always told, 'You're not smart. You need to change.' But there's always so much stuff. I didn't have the ability to shut it down." When I asked what he meant, he said the following:

One day, sitting in a college classroom, I left my body. Took an astral trip. It's embarrassing to talk about this. It was not drug induced. I went out the window, looking at the university, the city, the country, the planet. Looking at the earth from space I'm seeing all of everything connected. I could see the web of life; it was a moment of pure light. I thought it was a moment of clarity.

Tom could not slow his radiant rainforest mind down enough to get through college. There was just too much life in the jungle.

His painful experiences in school were still etched in his memory. He told me that I still had not convinced him that he had a rainforest mind:

I think I've stumbled through life to figure out how to perform certain functions with enough authority that I can be considered to be, at least, competent. I've fooled most everyone around me. You call that having a rainforest mind. So, I have fooled you, too.

I told Tom that I know one when I see one. After all, I had been hanging out with his kind for years. (Lucky me!) And I also recognized that RFMs know how much they do not know and often underestimate their abilities. But I hoped that, in time, I would convince him that success in school may not be an indicator of advanced intellect so he would gain the confidence he needed to recognize his strengths and appreciate his zeal—even if he still did not know his multiplication facts.

Will: Maximum Velocity

Will, 19, first called me and left a message saying that he had "lots of issues to figure out" and that he was dealing with both depression and anxiety. "I'm not sure if I need a counselor or a coach or both," he explained. In my return message, I offered a free 20-minute get-acquainted meeting to see whether we were a good match.

He arrived a bit late on his bike, a rangy young man wearing a T-shirt, jeans, and a sincere smile. I began by asking what brought him to counseling. As he talked about his depression and anxiety, he mentioned that he was going into his final year in college and would be going back to school in two weeks.

I could not imagine how we would approach Will's significant emotional issues in that length of time. I told him as much and that perhaps a coach would be more suitable. But he seemed to have determined already that I could help him. I decided to seek more information. If his issues were due to giftedness and not related to a dysfunctional family system, then I might be able to do some psycho-education that could have an impact, even in a couple of meetings. The situation was far from ideal, but it might be workable.

With our short timeline in mind, I asked Will if he had been identified as "talented and gifted" in school. He said "yes," but quickly added that he did not really know what it meant. He then said that he experienced anxiety around achievement in school and had been depressed off and on over the years—but he was unsure why. He described high standards and pressure that he put on himself. He said he would lose perspective when he would often "over-reach" on assignments and wondered if he might have ADHD.

Will wanted help understanding why he could "ace organic chemistry but fail the easy classes." He said he tried to do too much at once and then would get work in late because he couldn't focus and was disorganized. He claimed he didn't have great time management skills. He added that his parents, both accomplished geologists, were super supportive. "They believe in me but I worry about disappointing them."

Even though Will's symptoms might have looked like a classic case of ADHD, I wondered if, perhaps, what he really needed was an understanding of himself as a gifted person and specific information about perfectionism. Many gifted individuals have been misdiagnosed with ADHD. If a gifted student is failing classes, turning work in late, overwhelmed, and easily distracted, I check to see if the curriculum is appropriately stimulating and ask if, when he is interested in the subject or connecting well with the teacher, the problems are greatly reduced.

Additionally, I look for environments and circumstances in which the student is able to focus successfully. I have found that learning style can be a factor: Students with a more random and creative learning style actually do better working on more than one item at a time, but this can look disorganized and distracted.

We met again a few days later. Will had read the articles I had given him and said that he was astonished at how much he had in common with the gifted people profiled. We talked about the particular characteristics that many in this population exhibit. When I told him that he appeared to have most of these traits, he expressed discomfort with the label "gifted." So I explained the rainforest mind analogy.

This perspective resonated with Will. He went on to say, "I was a nerd in high school. Got perfect SAT scores but turned work in late because I tried to do too much. Fifth grade," he said, "was a time that shaped my worldview." He asked detailed questions, especially in science, that the teacher either would not answer directly or would totally ignore. He remembered numerous instances of being sent out of the classroom and being told that he had anger problems. I wondered if the teacher may not have known how to handle such intense curiosity and sharp intellect, and if Will got angry because he felt frustrated and rejected.

On the social front, Will felt lonely most of the time. He did not relate well to peers. When a child's chronological age is eight but his mental age is 14, for example, it is harder to connect with children of the same chronological age. I wondered if that was the case for Will, so I gave him examples of clients who had similar frustrations in school and difficulties finding friends. He was relieved to hear that he was not alone.

Ambitious Goals
Because we had so little time, Will and I focused more on recent experiences than on childhood issues. It was not hard for me to

see that he was intellectually advanced, based on the issues he was describing. But there was some harder evidence, too, such as his SAT scores, his interest in nanoscience, and the fact that he taught himself calculus when he needed it as a prerequisite for a class in college.

Will described "ambitious intellectual goals" and said that he had a double major in chemistry and geology, but he recently lost confidence and no longer felt any joy in learning. He explained, "I have a pattern of going at maximum velocity then running out of steam. I can't relax, I'm anxious about the future, and I'm generally overwhelmed because I over-think everything." I told him that the rainforest mind often runs nonstop, on more than one track at a time, and typically worries about the wellbeing of others and the planet. I told him that an 18-year-old girl I was seeing described how overwhelmed she felt by "the unbearable suffering in the world" and how she felt "desperate to take care of everyone." Her empathy was enormous. Will could relate.

The "velocity" that Will described can appear to counselors to resemble mania because it can be so energetic and intense. But I have found that it is not usually pathological. I told Will about another client who said she had made an agreement with her husband that when she was too overwhelming for him, kind of like a fire hose, he would say to her "garden hose, garden hose" and she would tone it down.

In our last session, Will and I explored how his rainforest mind was affecting his experience in college and how perfectionism might be playing a part. First, I suggested that his insatiable curiosity, his love of learning, and his enormous need for intellectual stimulation might be making it difficult for him to focus on completing assignments and keeping deadlines. His tendency to wander into other topics and do unending research was fed by these traits. In addition, for a mind that thrived on complexity, mundane tasks could be very difficult, almost painful, to complete. This helped him understand the paradox of getting the lower grades in easier subjects.

We discussed how Will might use self-talk to remind himself that his goal for school was to finish assignments and meet requirements, and that he needed to keep bringing himself back to the task and to keep it contained. He said, "I need to add more structure to my life. I stay more focused when I eat regularly, get enough sleep, and exercise every day. Yoga's very centering for me and I've always wanted to start a meditation practice."

I described how intrinsic perfectionism manifests in a rainforest mind and affects both major and minor decisions, word choice, assignments, relationships, and much more. What might be an easy process for someone else becomes a much bigger deal for the person who is on a quest for beauty or harmony. He smiled and nodded in agreement.

I suggested to Will that he assume that his yearning for perfection was not pathological. To be successful in school, though, he needed to learn to prioritize his activities and choose which situations warranted thoroughness and which ones to keep basic or minimal. I emphasized that he would not be compromising his values or idealism by doing this, which was a concern of his.

Will listened carefully and I could see the wheels turning. When I asked him what might help with this prioritizing, he said, "I'll create some artwork with these themes embedded in them. It'll be like propaganda to myself." Since he'd mentioned feeling connected to nature, I suggested that he find a rock or some other natural object to keep on his desk or carry with him that could remind him of his deeper purpose, so that he would feel more peaceful and able to readily connect with his authentic self.

Ten Thousand Species of Ants

I wanted to continue to explore Will's concerns but our time was up. With more time, I would have explored whether Will felt pressure from his family to be smart and to excel. I also would have referred him for an assessment for ADHD.

But we had made a start. For some clients needing to understand the complexities of their giftedness, even a few meetings may make a difference. And yet, we had barely entered the rain forest, just seen a couple of toucans and some exotic ferns. What about the ten thousand species of ants?

But Will looked ready to move on. He thanked me for the therapy with a slight tinge of surprise in his voice, as though he had not really expected to be helped. Then he said, "Thanks for the drive-by counseling," grinned, hopped on his bike, and rode off.

Strategies

✑ You may need help processing your schooling experiences. If you did not get good grades because you were disillusioned with the system or because of other RFM traits, you may have concluded that you were not too bright. Or you may have had good grades, but you were not particularly challenged or engaged in real learning, so you concluded that something was seriously wrong with you. Express your grief and anger with a friend or counselor who understands.

✑ Find ways to get intellectual stimulation. Go to lectures and art galleries, travel, read, take a scientist or an artist or a retired college professor to lunch. Learn a new language, study musical instruments. Look online for people and projects you can join.

✑ Let curiosity be your extreme sport.

✑ You may feel deep frustration with the whole idea of identifying and labeling children as "gifted" in school. You, or people you know, may have been overlooked because you or they did not fit a stereotype of smartness. Are there ways you can work within the system to change it? Can you research teaching models that differentiate learning for all kids in a classroom so assignments meet the individual needs of each child through more open-ended, interdisciplinary approaches? Can you get involved at your neighborhood school and volunteer in a classroom?

✑ Go to innovativelearningconference.org to connect with education innovators.

✑ Appreciate your sense of humor even if others do not. For some clever and wise philosophy, check out *Daily Afflictions: The Agony of Being Connected to Everything in the Universe*, by Andrew Boyd.

❧ Contact a former teacher who changed your life. Thank her or him.

❧ If you suspect that you might have ADHD, OCD, bipolar disorder, or a learning disability, do some research about the "twice exceptional" gifted adult and see what you find out. A good place to start is 2enewsletter.com, Diane Kennedy and Rebecca Banks' book *Bright Not Broken*, or additudemag.com

❧ Get out of the box, let go of normal, and stop trying to climb into the box.

❧ If you are looking for colleges that will meet your needs, check *Colleges that Change Lives*, by Loren Pope, and *Cool Colleges*, by Donald Asher. Once you are at college or university, find the professors who love your probing questions and meet with them during office hours. Let them help you get through the system. Take advantage of college counseling centers and academic advising.

❧ Read Tom Clynes' engaging book *The Boy Who Played With Fusion: Extreme Science, Extreme Parenting, And How To Make A Star*. Clynes is an articulate advocate for gifted kids struggling in the school system.

❧ Consider alternatives to the traditional schooling models for your RFM children. A great resource is giftedhomeschoolers.org. Go to their website and Facebook page for an abundance of ideas from parents who are making alternative education work. Look at their resources, books (GHF Press), and their blog hops for support for raising gifted kids. They also specialize in resources for twice exceptional children.

- Attend a SENG (Supporting the Emotional Needs of the Gifted) conference or your state TAG (Talented and Gifted) conference. Go to NAGC.org (National Organization for Gifted Children). Find great resources at hoagiesgifted.org website, Facebook page, and blog hops.

- Volunteer at your child's school and identify the teachers who would be good matches for your child. Get to know them.

- Redefine "geek." Try on Jon Katz's non-traditional definition from his book, *Geeks: How Two Lost Boys Rode the Internet out of Idaho*:

  > *Tendency toward braininess and individuality, traits that often trigger resentment, isolation, or exclusion. Identifiable by a singular obsessiveness about things they love, both work and play, and a well-honed sense of bitter, even savage, outsider humor. Universally suspicious of authority. In this era, the Geek Ascension, a positive, even envied term.*

Chapter Seven

Authenticity and Creativity and Spirituality, Oh My!

Science is not only compatible with spirituality; it is a profound source of spirituality.
~Carl Sagan[79]

The Search for Authenticity

Perhaps you are wondering how one chapter could possibly address authenticity, creativity, and spirituality, when each topic could fill volumes. The best response I can give is that I am focusing on the narrower topic of how having a rainforest mind might affect your thoughts about and experiences of these rather gigantic subjects, based on my years of experience with RFMs. It is anecdotal as seen through my own naturally biased lens. As with the rest of the book, I welcome your differing opinions and encourage you to accept what works for you and to leave the rest.

I wonder if much of your day-to-day motivation stems from your deep desire to live an honest, real, and meaningful life. You may go to great lengths to examine your actions, statements, emotions, and thoughts because you want to speak and live your truth. It really matters. This may be one of many occasions when you are told by others to lighten up or that you think too much. But you feel driven by the need to be authentic.

You may feel conflicted in situations where you slow down to be understood or where you are tempted to compromise to be part of a group. Perhaps you want to tell what you know about a topic or share a perception you have of a person or show all of your excitement about something new you have learned. This would be the real, authentic, uncensored you. But if you have frequently experienced others getting lost and overwhelmed in your enthusiasm or confused by your vocabulary, then you may feel that you have to grapple with a no-win choice—authenticity or inclusion.

A way to reframe this dilemma is that when you temper your intensity or slow your speech in order to communicate effectively, you do this consciously and as it makes sense for the particular situation. In that case, you are still being authentic, even though you are not saying everything you are thinking. (That would be impossible anyway, right?) And, if you have been raised in a dysfunctional home, you may make choices to protect parts of yourself when interacting with family members. This is not being inauthentic, either. You are making healthy choices for yourself and setting up appropriate boundaries. You are aware of what you are doing in these instances and making choices based on your truth and based on what, in your estimation, your listeners are capable of handling. While you want to be honest and open in your relationships, you may need to do some monitoring of communications so that your message is heard or so that you keep yourself safe.

All of these adaptations, then, are healthy and appropriate ways of improving your communication with others while remaining authentic. But what if you experience an ongoing authenticity challenge because you do not believe that you have a rainforest mind? What if, in fact, you suspect that if people knew the real you, they would see that you are good at faking intelligence and you have been fooling people all of these years? This belief is more common than you might imagine. It's called "impostor syndrome."[80]

Earlier in the book, I mentioned how RFMs know how much they do not know and often do not see themselves as all that smart.

They also assume that others have similar capacities and that these others just may not be applying themselves. This may be, in part, because you assume that what comes easily to the RFM must also be easy for others. But that is not the case. Understand that others may not be as capable as you are in certain—perhaps many—areas.

And that is not all. You may not value your work if you have not had to struggle to produce it; you may even feel guilty about it. For example, perhaps you write poetry or play a musical instrument or know several languages. For most people, mastery takes many rewrites or years of practice, but these abilities seem to flow through you and do not take much effort. How can you take credit, then, for something that comes naturally? So, either you minimize the extent of your capabilities because you believe that everyone has them, or you discount your talents out of embarrassment or because you do not believe you can take credit for them.[81]

As I mentioned in the chapter on perfectionism (Chapter Three), this natural ability may also mean that you expect everything you learn to come quickly and easily. When it does not, you conclude that you are not so smart after all. You do not realize that some things are supposed to be difficult. Not everything you try will be, or should be, easy to learn. Or, you may decide not to risk trying anything you are not sure you will do well, so as not to expose your deficiencies. The complexity of these issues makes it hard to sort yourself out, much less explain yourself to others. Adrienne, an effervescent client, said she felt her academic successes were due to luck and being liked by her teachers. She called being an A student her "comfort object," like an intangible stuffed animal, and she constantly worried she would be exposed as a fraud.

Authenticity and the Dysfunctional Family

You may have other reasons why you do not feel so smart. If you grew up in a family with emotional, physical, or sexual abuse or neglect, your perception of who you are has been distorted by the behaviors and beliefs of your parents and other family members. When we are young, we cannot understand the reasons why we are being mistreated. We usually blame ourselves and start to form our sense of self based on these distortions.[82]

As adults, we may continue to feel unworthy or unlovable, even if we achieve what others would evaluate as success. As a result, we experience a disconnection between who we feel we are and who we really are. We might get positive feedback from friends about their impressions of our fabulousness. But we do not believe it. We feel inauthentic.

Being an RFM means that these effects are probably both more and less intense. You probably noticed more and felt more, but you also may have understood at an early age that the dysfunction was not your fault. An inner guidance system probably made you more resilient. Even so, your journey toward self-actualization will take time, gentleness, multiple methods, and patience. Even though you are a fast learner, processing childhood wounds is not academic learning. But it is worthwhile, and you will find many rewards along the way.

If this is your story, one way to find your true Self again is to engage a good therapist and work through your past experiences until you are able to recognize your radiance. I know I have mentioned this many times throughout this book, and you might say I have a bit of a bias. If I do, it is because I have seen the life-enhancing impact of good psychotherapy over and over again.

Therapy could take some time if you are the type of person who is deep and thorough, which is likely, because of your RFM. Sometimes therapy can feel like "Diving into the Wreck," the title of a poem by Adrienne Rich. I believe that finding your true voice and living your real life is among the most important work you can do.

If your quest for authenticity continues to be a tricky business, there is a study that demonstrates that RFMs do not recognize the extent of their strengths. In the *Journal of Personality and Social Psychology*, Kruger and Dunning learned that "unskilled individuals suffer from illusory superiority," while brighter people underestimate their skills.[83]

Or, as Shakespeare wrote in *As You Like It*, "The fool doth think he is wise, but the wise man knows himself to be a fool."

Authenticity Meets Creativity Meets Spirituality

Interestingly, as you grapple with living your authentic life, you may find your creativity to be both a problem and a solution. Being a divergent thinker or coming up with creative ideas often means that you are not a part of the norm, and, in some cases it can get you rejected and ridiculed. But if, as the author Pearl Buck said, you feel "the overpowering necessity to create, create, create" then, you must do it. She adds, "[W]ithout the creating of music or poetry or books or buildings or something of meaning, his very breath is cut off from him . . . he is not really alive unless he is creating."[84]

Your creativity, then, becomes an expression of your authenticity. Steven Pressfield adds, "Our job in this lifetime is not to shape ourselves into some ideal we imagine we ought to be, but to find out who we already are and become it."[85] Not an easy job when you have so many choices and so many layers. But it is something you must do. This is why I connect authenticity with creativity and spirituality. I find that they all dance together in a dynamic tango—or is that a tangle?

While you want to become your real self and you are called to create, where might spirituality come in?

I have worked with many RFMs seeking some sort of religious or spiritual direction. Instead, they find frustration. Finding one religion or spiritual path that meets your needs may be difficult. Typically, RFMs are searching for meaning and are skeptical of easy answers. They may be drawn to spiritual mysteries and have experiences that cannot be easily explained rationally or they may only find peace in the natural world.[86]

While you may yearn for spiritual community, it may be hard to find. Researcher and education professor Jane Piirto explains:

With their verbal facility, capacity for abstract thinking, and ability to understand complexity, gifted and talented adults often find traditional religion wanting, especially religion of the fundamentalist sort. They struggle to reconcile dogma with faith, belief with proof, and their minds often overrule their emotions in the struggle. Many leave traditional churches and may take up other religions. . . . Alternative spiritual paths beckon, or they may not embrace any spirituality at all, so troubling is the requirement for conformity in traditional religions.[87]

In spite of the challenge, I have found a common thread among many of my clients: a sense of peace and spirit in nature. Sometimes they have an affinity with Buddhism and/or mindfulness practices, or contemplative religious organizations. Annemarie Roeper described a student she knew who had a rock collection who said he felt the aliveness of each rock and of the Earth as a whole. She repeatedly met children who had an "expanded experience of reality."[88] When Barbara Kerr wrote about her apprenticeship with a Native American shaman, she talked of "layers of realities, with different ways of knowing at each level."[89]

While Kerr found layers, Michael Piechowski, molecular biologist and counseling psychologist, looked at themes. He studied adults who reported spiritual experiences as children and found that certain categories were repeated: "unity, oneness [with nature], timelessness, or the interconnection of everything." Other common experiences included visions of "pulsing light" and of a "powerful divine loving energy." Among his interviewees, he also noticed a high incidence of "entelechy": the drive to find one's purpose and to live it fully.[90]

David James Duncan, author of *The River Why*, found his purpose and serenity in the natural world from a very early age:

In even the smallest suburban wilds I felt linked to powers and mysteries I could sincerely imagine calling the Presence of God . . .

Following intuition and love with all the sincerity and attentiveness I could muster, I consciously chose a life spent in the company of rivers, wilderness, Wisdom literature, like-minded friends, and quiet contemplation. And as it's turned out, this life—though dirt-poor in church pews—has enriched me with a sense of the holy, and left me far more grateful than I'll ever be able to say.[91]

Roeper noted how the children she taught seemed to connect to a larger sense of what is real. Children would talk to her about their experiences of the connections between everything and of a living Earth. Their experiences included "ESP, memories of previous lives, déjà vu experiences, and prenatal memories."[92] Author Elaine Aron agrees and includes "visions, voices, or miracles, and . . . intimate personal relationships with God, angels, saints, or spirit guides,"[93] as she explains how highly sensitive people might be particularly "soulful and spiritual."[94]

Psychologist Patricia Gatto-Walden has studied spirituality in gifted adults. She described "heightened spirituality" as:

[P]rofound sensitivity and compassion, depth of empathy, integrity, honesty, intuitive inner guidance, living in accordance with equality and justice, and an ability to move beyond everyday reality into oneness with God, nature, the universe, or "All That Is."[95]

Gatto-Walden's clients described experiences such as:

[C]ommunication with angels, nature, animals, plants, and stars or . . . experiences of transcendence of an expansive universe or God . . . knowing that a pervasive, all-encompassing love binds together the self to all of life and connects the self in the present and beyond.[96]

Kathleen Noble, scholar and author, described a near-death experience that altered her sense of reality and led her to study the topic of spiritual intelligence. She explained:

> *And I was reminded that we are never truly alone. Not only does there exist an immense network of intelligent and loving allies who sustain and support us as we struggle to grow, but also some portion of our larger self always comprehends what we are doing and where we are heading. No matter where we might find ourselves in the vast complexity of the whole, there is always a level of awareness that is old enough and smart enough to understand. And I was shown that each of us, no matter how small or insignificant we might sometimes feel, is vital to the whole, to a depth and degree we are wont to forget.*[97]

The Many Forms of Spirituality

It's hard for me to talk about spirituality without worrying that I sound self-righteous, out of my league, or, as a teenage client of mine called me once "too frou-frou." So, I admit, right now, to you, dear reader, that I am all of those things. But I just cannot leave this part out.

I recently discovered a book titled *Belonging Here: A Guide for the Spiritually Sensitive Person*, by Judith Blackstone. Through her own painful personal process of healing and self-actualization, Blackstone developed a program called the Realization Process that carefully takes highly sensitive people into their bodies to discover their spirituality, their luminosity, and to learn how to live as embodied spirit in what she calls "fundamental consciousness." Her characteristics of spiritual sensitivity overlap many of those of the rainforest mind, such as "heightened perception, abundant energy, exceptional emotional depth, or the ability to see into the truth of situations."[98] The exercises in her books provide another way to walk through the doorway to your Self.

My client, Janice (Chapter One) described her embodied experience of her essence or true Self, which she called her "bedrock":

Even now, I can feel the bedrock in my body. The bedrock offers no judgment and no anger or resentment. It simply knows that to be fully embodied, you must follow the truth it sets out for you. By connecting with it, it simply fills me with the undeniable notion that I know what to do. And I can get it done. . . . It's knowing that, through the highs and lows of the creative process, you can move forward and continue to grow through adversity. And it's the best feeling I've ever discovered.

Spirituality comes in many forms. Noble says, "[T]he mystical is in the moment, and we live there all the time." We just need to remember who we really are. Her research into spiritual intelligence supports the belief in the potential for humans to "evolve a new paradigm of morality that enables us to live in greater harmony with all beings."[99] The possibility of new levels of deep harmony and all of the spirituality research I have mentioned is what keeps me feeling hopeful about our future.

Many RFMs have their own, idiosyncratic way of contacting spirituality. My client, Gene, follows the "School of Wandering Aimlessly in Nature." How about you? What mystery calls your name?

Steven: Lost and Found

Steven, 34, came to see me for a consultation because his 10-year-old son, Tim, was having difficulty in school. A counselor at a summer camp told Steven that his son was gifted and suggested that he see me. Tim had not been identified as gifted in school, but was labeled ADHD and seen as a troublemaker. Steven said that he needed help speaking with school personnel and also needed parenting guidance.

Steven described Tim's defiant behaviors at school: refusing to do assignments and arguing with other children. He also misbehaved at home and Steven's authoritarian responses were ineffective. Steven was a single parent and Tim's mom had a drug addiction which kept her from being a regular presence in his life. Steven had a stressful job in the engineering field and difficulty with relationships with women, in which he often ended up feeling "used and overwhelmed."

We worked first on strategizing ways that Steven could communicate more effectively with Tim, using active listening and "I" messages. I suggested that some of Tim's anger might stem from feeling abandoned by his mother. We also looked at Tim's schooling situation and how Steven might ask Tim's teacher to refer him for testing to see if he was in the gifted range. Since I did not see youngsters Tim's age for counseling, I referred him to a colleague and recommended books for Steven to read about giftedness in children, including Sally Walker's *The Survival Guide for Parents of Gifted Kids*.

It became apparent to me that Steven would also benefit from counseling. He had shared that his father had been verbally and physically abusive and had molested his sister. His parents had divorced when he was nine and his mother had left him with his father. Steven had felt abandoned. During high school, he used drugs, skipped classes, and dropped out. His own anger could be triggered by his son's defiant behaviors, and his fury was out of proportion to the situation.

I suspected that Steven also was an RFM from the insightful way he communicated his thoughts and feelings and from how he had educated himself to reach a high-powered career as a civil engineer. I asked him to consider this possibility and described the typical traits so that he could apply them both to his son and himself. Steven responded with a description of a creative side of himself that he felt had been lost. He loved writing fantasy stories and playing Dungeons and Dragons, but had limited those activities after the birth of his son. He also missed hiking and kayaking.

After several sessions on parenting techniques and family history, I decided that Steven might be a good candidate for guided imagery work with an inner child. In fact, he was quite receptive and was able to visualize a vulnerable little boy fairly easily, centered in his heart. Steven was tearful as he said, "Pure light flows through him. He's not tainted." This was an important realization that allowed Steven to start on the road to self-acceptance.

As we continued with the guided imagery, Steven was able to feel his grief for the losses that had occurred during his childhood along with the joy that this small inner child still held. On one occasion, he felt like he had connected with a higher Self through the visualization and he began to meditate at home to strengthen this experience. Over time, he was able to tune into his higher Self when he was with Tim so that their exchanges were more loving.

Steven reported progress in his relationship with Tim. He found that when he listened carefully and stayed calm, Tim became vulnerable and expressed his fears and concerns openly and without anger. Realizing that his son was very bright helped Steven better understand Tim's reactions and sensitivities as well as his own. Things also improved at school. Tim was calmer and teachers were more receptive to providing some alternative assignments.

Steven was able to set healthy boundaries with his son so that he could have time to develop his creative interests, particularly his interest in writing fantasy. This, in turn, made him more open to taking time to hike and give his son the loving attention that Steven had never received from his own father. He had finally rediscovered his creativity and spiritual center through his connection with the light-filled, joyful boy hidden for so long in his heart.

Eli: Slow Down, Tune In

Eli, 46, was an earnest, inquisitive, high school math teacher who came to counseling for "mid-life depression, marital struggles, and anxiety." He was also having some physical problems that he suspected were the result of unresolved issues from his past. He had been reading the psychotherapist Carl Jung and wondering whether there might be a way to open to a more spiritual side of himself.

I began by describing the characteristics of the RFM. In response, Eli shared that he was highly sensitive. For example, he said that he had to stop himself from crying at a recent student choir and band performance when he was deeply moved by the quality of the performances and the beauty of the music. He experienced himself as intense, intuitive, and perfectionistic.

In examining his childhood, Eli uncovered shame, repressed anger, and deep grief as he realized how much of his authentic self he had needed to hide in order to survive his alcoholic family. With counseling, he allowed himself to grieve these losses and, through guided visualization, reconnected with his child self whom he came to see as a fabulously sensitive, exuberant being. In one visualization, he saw his five-year-old self, shirtless on his bike, chatting with the neighbors who obviously liked him. In a moment of joy, he exclaimed tearfully, "What a beautiful animal!"

Eli was wondering how he might expand into a more spiritual consciousness. We talked about meditation, including books to read and how he might look for classes or conferences that taught this practice. In the meantime, we did some guided imagery looking for his inner guidance and, when placing his hand over his heart and tuning into himself, he felt a connection with something profound and deep that moved him to tears. We did this in a few more sessions; each time, Eli touched into something sacred in himself.

On one occasion, he described a "benevolent voice" inside which told him, "It's OK, you didn't understand" and "You don't have to try so hard." He said when he tuned into this deep, authentic Self, he could "see the beauty of existence" and that his heart understood "the human condition." The last time we talked, he reported much less anxiety, more spontaneity, and a deep sense of peace and well-being whenever he slowed down and tuned in. His beautiful animal was released!

Beverly: Awakening

Beverly, 38, was an animated, expressive woman. She was referred to me by her couples counselor. I was facilitating groups for gifted women at the time and her counselor recognized her giftedness and suspected that Beverly would benefit from meeting intellectual peers. Beverly had read widely about giftedness and had more awareness than most about how her rainforest mind impacted choices, her relationships, and career path.

Beverly wanted to focus on understanding how her childhood experiences were being played out in her partnership and how she might bring any unhealthy patterns to light so that she could be less reactive when familiar, painful feelings and thoughts were triggered. She and her partner, Melody, worked hard in couples counseling and generally had good communication skills and a loving connection.

Over the first several weeks, Beverly painted a picture of her early years. She described both her mixed feelings about being a gifted child and her perceptions of her parents and her two younger sisters. Some themes emerged. In school, Beverly felt out of sync with the other children and had difficulty finding friends. Her love of intellectual pursuits, especially reading at an early age, was not shared or appreciated by her peers. She was ostracized and bullied. She remembered raising her hand when she knew an answer and seeing other children glaring at her, when she was "just trying to do the right thing."

Her enthusiasm for learning got mixed reviews at home, as well. Her mother, while expressing pride in her child's accomplishments some of the time, would also warn her against being too proud of herself or enjoying her achievements too much.

"I could sense my mother's discomfort. She was threatened by my giftedness," Beverly explained. She took these warnings to heart and felt guilty, embarrassed, and confused if she excelled academically. She got the message that while she may be smart, she should not acknowledge it because she would hurt others if she did.

Both of Beverly's parents were often anxious and fearful, which would then be felt and misinterpreted by sensitive Beverly as something that she did wrong and needed to fix. Even though both of Beverly's parents communicated a certain amount of loving attention, they also seemed somewhat self-absorbed. In fact, her mother had some difficulty separating her needs from her daughter's and would often rely on Beverly in a way that was both passive-aggressive and childlike.

Tension would build because her mother did not know how to communicate her concerns in a healthy way. She directed angry outbursts at her children without telling them why she was upset. As a result, Beverly developed a deep, lasting fear of doing the wrong thing and making the wrong decision.

As we uncovered these experiences and issues, Beverly had a hard time feeling compassion for herself since there had been no obvious abuse in her home. Her basic needs were met and her parents loved her. While these more subtle dysfunctional patterns are common, I find that they often need to be explained so that clients can understand the source of their present distress while maintaining an appreciation for the caring they did receive. Beverly described her experience this way:

> The *most important authenticity issue for me is I'm always good.* *Even someone who doesn't have obvious abuse can still come out feeling not good. It's from feeling different. My natural abilities threatening others. A school system that sets children against each other creates competition by expecting them to do the same thing at the same time.*

As Beverly grew more comfortable in counseling, she told me about an experience of sexual abuse while living at a spiritual center after college. The memories of ongoing abuse by the leader of the center brought back feelings of fear, shame, and anger. Off and on during our time together, we processed these events so that Beverly could grieve the resulting losses and repair any sense of self-blame.

In working with the themes from childhood, Beverly responded well to visualization. She had already established a relaxation technique that created a safe place in her psyche. After she contacted that place, I would guide her to visit with an inner child who needed her attention and compassion. Over time, Beverly was able to appreciate the child's sensitivity and curiosity and accept her confused, scared feelings. We also worked on ways Beverly could comfort her child self without becoming overwhelmed by her emotions. In this way, Beverly was giving herself the attention, understanding, consistency, and boundaries that she needed.

Finding Inner Wisdom

Beverly worked at home and had a successful career as an editor. She was also an accomplished artist, selling and showing her art, as well as teaching classes. Over the time she was in counseling, she started learning guitar and created a band that performed in local venues around town. She and Melody adopted and raised a daughter. Melody ran a small nonprofit and Beverly joined the board and helped with logistics now and then. She often had new career ideas and kept a journal of many possible projects that she might never have the time to do. She had read Sher's *Refuse to Choose* and worked with her online and at conferences.

Whenever Beverly became deeply involved in one of her many interests, she became fearful that she would not get back to the others. She created a solution to this problem by visualizing a large house with many rooms. Each room contained a project or interest. When she was in one of the rooms, she could relax in the confidence of knowing that all of her other projects were available even if she was currently focused on just one.

One of Beverly's goals in counseling was to identify past experiences that had distorted her view of herself and then find her true nature, her authenticity, and live a creative, compassionate life. Developing her creative voice was particularly important:

> *Creativity is one of my big struggles. I spent my whole first year in therapy getting myself to draw, finding triggers blocking me from expressing my creativity. I passionately wanted to do visual art and I wasn't able to. The fear of disapproval, fear of expressing my true self in the world because at the root I believed I was bad.*

Fear of doing the wrong thing. All stopped me from drawing. Trusting and valuing my core self gave me the confidence to draw. Then art fell to the side and music came and brought me back to the damn beginning. I'm going through the same process with song writing!

Beverly knew that support from others was particularly important to her. She found such a community at a website, fluentself.com, where Havi Brooks teaches playful, self-accepting methods for recognizing triggers, getting unstuck and rewriting patterns. One of the most powerful techniques for Beverly was similar to Richard Schwartz's Internal Family Systems therapy. Written conversations with parts of herself (who received names like the "Responsibility Child" and "Wrong Thing Me") led to deeper awareness and transformed some of the old patterns. Sharing her process and observing others helped Beverly feel held and seen in her inner work.

Beverly shared some of her dialogues in our sessions and would talk about her "Awake Me" as a part that provided much insight. When I heard the loving messages from Awake Me about trust, opening to joy, and being in the present moment, I suggested to Beverly that she had accessed her true Self and that as she talked with that Self, she would get what she needed. As her Awake Me wrote, "[T]rust isn't about gathering all your strength and taking a big leap across a chasm. . . . Trust is really about knowing there is no chasm. There is no other side. You're already there."

Strategies

ᔓ Read Kathleen Nobles's *Riding the Windhorse: Spiritual Intelligence and the Growth of the Self* to get inspiration and direction. She says:

> *Spiritual intelligence can only be achieved by expanding our psychological breadth and depth, living more deliberately, and functioning more wholly as individuals and in the world. Further, one must choose to perceive everyone and everything as more than meets the eye and choose to consciously align one's behavior with that awareness.*[100]

ᔓ Spend time in nature. Have conversations with places, trees, rocks, birds, and the rest of the "more than human world" (an expression from David Abram). Start a praise practice, giving thanks to the souls in nature. (See Bill Plotkin's *Nature and the Human Soul* for details.) Let the natural world show you how to live.

ᔓ If you were raised in a religious tradition that is still important to you, explore it more deeply. Don't remain satisfied with the information and understanding from your childhood, but use your RFM to go deeper into the tradition. You may find depths that continue to resonate, or you may realize that this is not the spiritual path you find fulfilling. But explore before you leave.

ᔓ Seek out a spiritual advisor in your religious tradition. This may be someone in about the same place as you with whom you can explore together, or someone ahead of you who can give you direction, or someone trained to offer guidance.

ᔓ Anne Lamott's books of essays are uplifting, funny, and inspiring.

ᔓ Make art. Use whatever tools feel good: pencils, paints, clay, pens. Go to your local art supply store and see what materials call out to you. Even if you are not artistically adept, you may enjoy making very simple art journals. Consider including collage, writing, and mementos to express your emotions and find your authentic voice.

๑๑ Build your own personal therapeutic deck of cards, using Seena Frost's book, *Soul Collage*.

๑๑ Shop around for a therapist who has done, and is still doing, his/her own inner work, and who knows something about giftedness (or is willing to learn). Include body workers, acupuncturists, ministers, rabbis, and imams, if you want to approach healing from multiple directions.

๑๑ In *The Highly Sensitive Person*, Elaine Aron describes the types of psychotherapies and how they work. She recommends a depth approach with aspects of other therapies as adjuncts.

๑๑ Build or strengthen a spiritual or self-care practice. Consider the possibility that you have a way to access guidance that is more loving and compassionate than your cognitive mind can grasp and that it will help you to find your true Self. Depending on your interests, check out books by Bill Plotkin, Jean Houston, Carl Sagan, C.S. Lewis, or Robert Moss.

๑๑ Read books by Judith Blackstone, particularly *Belonging Here: A Guide for the Spiritually Sensitive Person* and *The Subtle Self: Personal Growth and Spiritual Practice*. If you like what you read, attend one of her workshops.

๑๑ Explore the resources at The Institute of the Noetic Sciences at noetic.org. Read books by the Dalai Lama and Alan Watts. Explore an earth-centered spirituality through the work of Sandra Ingerman. Read Barbara Kerr's book, *Letters to the Medicine Man*.

ॐ Keep searching for yourself. Do as much therapy, reading, writing, obsessing, questioning, crying, analyzing, creating, dancing, exercising, building, snowboarding, and rebelling as you need to do to get to what feels like your soul's song. Then sing it. No matter what anyone tells you, sing out. The Universe will thank you.

ॐ Finally, understand and appreciate your rainforest mind so that you can, more happily and effectively, do what you are here to do.

Chapter Eight

Stop the Deforestation

We stand on the threshold of a great unknown. Individually and collectively, we launch into an uncertain future—at once, both perilous and saturated with possibility. Our accustomed, culturally-determined roles and identities are inadequate to navigate the sea change of our time. Our collective journey requires a radical shift in the human relationship with the community of all life—a cultural transformation so profound that future humans might regard it as an evolution of consciousness. Safe passage requires each of us to offer our full magnificence to the world.

~Animas Valley Institute[101]

In a 2008 op-ed column in *The New York Times*, Nicholas Kristof quoted novelist William Burroughs, who wrote that "intellectuals are deviants in the US."[102] Writer Burkhard Bilger, in a 2004 article in *The New Yorker* entitled "Nerd Camp," added, "Bright kids are used to fending for themselves in America. Dweeb, dork, brainiac, nerd: to be young and brilliant here is almost always to be a figure of some derision, to accept isolation as a condition of existence."[103]

And it does not end with childhood.

That said, I wonder if RFMs would say that even with the isolation, ridicule, sensitivities, and despair, they would still rather be gifted.

Maybe.

Speaking with the mother of one of my teen clients, I suspected that she was not so sure. Her daughter, Maggie, never fit well in a regular classroom with her same-aged peers. Year after year, school had been a nightmare. She did not think of herself as gifted and, in her desire for equality and justice for all, was offended by people who did. Maggie, now 18, still has frequent intense emotional meltdowns. Friends do not stay around long because Maggie wants to talk philosophy and Spanish literature when they, well, do not.

Maggie was desperately searching for intellectual stimulation, or at least for some teachers who could appreciate her zeal for research and debate. At the same time, she was terrified that if her schoolwork was challenging, she would fail miserably. She lived with the heavy weight of expectations imposed by her visions of perfection and her need to make a positive impact. She hid excessive self-doubt and shame as she repeatedly procrastinated on important assignments.

While Maggie found the spirituality of the ocean astounding when she allowed her sensitivities free rein, her empathy tended to overwhelm her nervous system. Nothing was uncomplicated. Even my description of her does not begin to explain her abundant, fertile, and tangled layers. Maggie's mother was exhausted and fearful for her daughter's future. They both wondered if being gifted was really such a gift.

But that is why I wrote this book. For Maggie, for her mom, and for all of you sweet "deviants." Do not give up. The planet cannot afford to lose any more of its rain forests.

Sadly, we did lose Aaron Swartz.

I heard about Aaron Swartz when I was glancing at CNN's website. He committed suicide at the age of 26. He was described as a prodigy who was idealistic, intense, empathic, funny, creative, curious, brilliant, and depressed. He was arrested in 2011 and accused of "using

MIT's computers to gain illegal access to millions of scholarly papers" to distribute them free of charge online.[104] It was reported that the prosecutors wanted to impose a harsh sentence to discourage computer crime.[105] Swartz had been involved with organizations fighting internet censorship and was "working on fixing US politics" by changing the way campaigns are funded.[106]

In an interview, Swartz said that he was not particularly smart or talented, just curious, and that his curiosity led him to find all things "interesting."[107] It is unclear what drove him to suicide. But reading about him, I cannot help wondering if the likely combination of factors included the burden of his rainforest mind. I wonder whether the depression he wrote about long before the incident was connected to his extreme sensitivity and his deep concern for justice.

There is much debate about whether gifted individuals are more vulnerable to suicide. Child psychologist Maureen Neihart has worked for years with gifted children. Her review of the literature suggests that they are not. But, toward the end of one article, she adds that, more specifically, it can depend on "the type of giftedness, the educational fit, and one's personal characteristics."[108] So, I wonder.

Granted, my view is skewed by the fact that most of the RFMs I have known over recent years have been therapy clients, individuals who have identified themselves as troubled in some way, so I do not have a fair sample from which to draw strong conclusions. Nonetheless, the rain forest is fragile as well as powerful, sensitive as well as lively and, in more and more places, gone.

Shall we end the clear-cutting now?

Crystalline Structures

You are made of crystalline structures,
that vibrate like tuning forks.
Their delicate iridescent wings
unfurl and lift them high on the soft breeze
of night to gather subtle informations
which few can understand.

You inhabit these *in formations*
Gathering them in tenderly and transposing them
when needed to harmonize the infinite tangled
song strands of earth.

Perhaps you ought to wear a helmet
and goggles in the shopping mall or
wrap your selves in blankets hung with
　　spells and crystals
Just to navigate the realm of ambient noise at work.

When the luminous wings of your soul flap,
you lift up out of ordinary time and immerse
yourself in beauty, or sorrow, or fierce love.
Whatever is before you, you enter and allow
the exquisite dilemma of life to welcome you
toward the Divine.

This is hard to accomplish at gas stations, bars
or gaming arcades. Also,
hospital waiting rooms, school cafeterias,
truck stops, cocktail parties or
among the very rich.

Naturally, you seek moving water, wetlands full

of water fowl and the cascade of crimson leaves.
Some cathedrals and Japanese garden shrines and
The company of your own   *strange   sort.*

None of this is easy. You must be an *ardent scientist
of replenishment.* You must be
the crafty, shape-shifting magician, just to whisk yourself
into psychic obscurity   at the right moment.

Certain sounds are helpful; the plunk and fall of water.
The early morning bird calls, the crackle of fire
against star light.
A gentle heart-felt chanting can lower the curtain
Of protection   around   your ears.

No one loves to cloak them selves more:
The soft fall of the cloth that makes you separate.
The eye lids of the soul, allowed to close.
The petals holding the bud.
The silk lantern wrapped around   the lilting light.

Do not listen to the harsh instructions of the world
which might delude you into using
what is odd and fragile and capable of magic
as an inadequate tool for bludgeoning.
Or spend *what you have*, for endurance.
Or to mire that intricate knowing
into covert arguments about power.

Allow yourself to float the billowy cape
of rose petals and golden leaves around you.
Turn away from those unhelpful influences.

Come towards the light, the beautiful night sky

Milky Way spiral of your soul.

You have lost so much to buy this sensitivity.

Protect it like the multifaceted jewel that she is.
Wrap that tuning fork in velvet and
  rock it to sleep at night.
Sing love songs and lullabies to those wispy neurons,
those singed nerve endings, those antennae
you attempted to hide under your hair.

You are made for healing.

So many lifetimes you must have prayed for this.
So many languages to mend the fabric
of the world
come from your deepest heart.

Oh, sing the melody of the spheres that you were meant
  to hold.
Sing the songs that weave the balance.
This color strand light weaving dance that *you* can do.

And let go.

Of needing to be rich or strong enough
to endure shopping malls or television.

Let the joy of who you are rise up,
a flowering light from the inside.
And only laugh and turn away   when anyone
would measure you in money or endurance

For what is endurance when you have fractured

and re-joined 1000 lifetimes?
Carried on your own laughter…
And the musical sounds of beauty and luminous
Hope!

© Anne Allanketner, *Spells of Mending*, (Soul Talk Poetry Press, 2009)

Recommended Resources

Introduction

Chapter One: Too Much: Intensity, Sensitivity, Empathy

Books

The Anxiety and Phobia Workbook, Edmund Bourne

Belonging Here, Judith Blackstone

The Body Keeps the Score: Brain, Mind, And Body in the Healing of Trauma, Bessel Van Der Kolk

Energy Medicine: Balancing your Body's Energies for Optimal Health, Donna Eden

The Gifted Adult, Mary-Elaine Jacobsen

Healing Through the Dark Emotions, Miriam Greenspan

The Highly Sensitive Person, Elaine Aron

The "I" of the Beholder: A Guided Journey to the Essense of a Child, Annemarie Roeper

Living with Intensity, Susan Daniels and Michael Piechowski, eds.

Misdiagnosis and Dual Diagnosis of Gifted Children and Adults, James Webb, et al

The Mood Cure, Julia Ross

A Natural History of the Senses, Diane Ackerman

The Post-Traumatic Stress Disorder Sourcebook, Glenn Schiraldi

Online

heartmath.org: Tools for health and well-being

noetic.org: The Institute of Noetic Sciences, studies consciousness and human potential

quietrev.com: Susan Cain's website on introversion

rainforestmind.wordpress.com/2014/09/07/empathy-gifted-adults/

rainforestmind.wordpress.com/2015/02/05/smart-sensitive-men/

rainforestmind.wordpress.com/2015/12/16/overexcitabilities-gifted-adults/

selfleadership.org: The internal family systems therapy model
soundstrue.com: Many resources for emotional and spiritual growth
traumahealing.org: Psychologist Peter Levine's work on somatic therapy

Chapter Two: If You're So Smart, Why Aren't You Saving the World?
Books

Active Hope: How to Face the Mess We're in Without Going Crazy, Joanna Macy
Daily Afflictions, Andrew Boyd
I Am Malala: The Girl Who Stood Up For Education and Was Shot by the Taliban, Malala Yousafzai
It's Not the End of the World: Developing Resilience in Times of Change, Joan Borysenko
A Path Appears: Transforming Lives, Creating Opportunity, Nicholas Kristof and Sheryl WuDunn
The More Beautiful World Our Hearts Know is Possible, Charles Eisenstein
This Changes Everything, Naomi Klein
Trauma Stewardship: An Everyday Guide to Caring for Self While Caring for Others, Laura Van Dernoot Lipsky, and Connie Burk
Wild Mind: A Field Guide to the Human Psyche, Bill Plotkin

Online

350.org: Environmentalist organization
animas.org: Programs supporting mental health through nature-based retreats
avaaz.org: International online activist organization
billmoyers.com: Bill Moyers, journalist
freethechildren.org: A child-centered international organization focused on poverty
janegoodall.org: Jane Goodall's global conservation organization
joannamacy.net: Joanna Macy, environmental activist
pemachodronfoundation.org: Pema Chodron, Buddhist nun
rainforestmind.wordpress.com/2014/06/21/still-sleepless-cranky-and-annoying-after-all-these-years/
wildethics.org: Alliance for Wild Ethics, David Abram director, author

Chapter Three: Perfectionism, Precision, Procrastination
Books
Bright Not Broken: Gifted Kids, ADHD, and Autism, Diane Kennedy and Rebecca Banks
Delivered From Distraction, Ed Hallowell and John Ratey

Fail Fast, Fail Often, Ryan Babineaux and John Krumboltz
Mindset, Carol Dweck
Presence: Bringing Your Boldest Self to Your Biggest Challenges, Amy Cuddy
Procrastination: Why You Do it, What to do about it NOW, Jane Burka and Lenora Yuen
The Secret Thoughts of Successful Women, Valerie Young
The War of Art, Steven Pressfield

Online

giftedchallenges.blogspot.com/2015/11/why-do-smart-women-forego-success.html
impostorsyndrome.com: Valerie Young author on impostor syndrome
journaltherapy.com: Kathleen Adams on journaling
rainforestmind.wordpress.com/2014/04/23/perfectionism-procrastination-and-perspicacity/
rainforestmind.wordpress.com/2014/05/06/perfectionisms-twin-sister/
ted.com/talks/amy_cuddy_your_body_language_shapes_who_you_are:
    Amy Cuddy's TED talk related to impostor syndrome

Chapter Four: Too Many Possibilities, Too Many Choices
Books

And What Do You Do? 10 Steps to Creating a Portfolio Career, Hopson and Ledger
Crossing the Unknown Sea: Work as a Pilgrimage of Identity, David Whyte
Finding Your Way in a Wild New World, Martha Beck
Free Range Humans, Marianne Cantwell
Rebels at Work, Lois Kelly and Carmen Medina
Refuse to Choose, Barbara Sher
Soul Collage, Seena Frost
The Renaissance Soul, Margaret Lobenstein
Zen and the Art of Making a Living, Laurence Boldt

Online

empoweryou.com: Laurence Boldt career guidance
giftedchallenges.blogspot.com/2014/10/stress-management-toolbox-nine-tips-for.html
marthabeck.com: Coaching and career guidance, books and workshops
noksnauta.nl/english.html: Noks Nauta's research on gifted adults and work
puttylike.com: Emilie Wapnick on multipotentiality

puttylike.com/whats-the-difference-between-add-and-multipotentiality/
rainforestmind.wordpress.com/2016/01/01/afflicted-with-too-much-talent/
TED.com: Inspirational ideas from speakers around the world

Chapter Five: Going It Alone
Books

Bright Adults: Uniqueness and Belonging across the Lifespan, Ellen Fiedler

Far From the Tree, Andrew Solomon

Getting the Love You Want, Harville Hendrix

Hold Me Tight: Seven Conversations for a Lifetime of Love, Sue Johnson

Love Cycles: The Five Essential Stages of Lasting Love, Linda Carroll

Off the Charts: Asynchrony and the Gifted Child, Christine Neville, Michael Piechowski, and Stephanie Tolan, eds.

Perfect Love, Imperfect Relationships, John Welwood

Quiet: The Power of Introverts in a World That Can't Stop Talking, Susan Cain

The Relationship Cure, John Gottman

Writing Your Own Script: A Parent's Role in the Gifted Child's Social Development, Corin Barsily Goodwin and Mika Gustavson

Online

giftedchallenges.blogspot.com/2015/07/gifted-adults-and-relationships-ten.html

giftedchallenges.blogspot.com/2015/07/gifted-adults-key-questions-that-can.html

gottman.com: John Gottman, psychologist

rainforestmind.wordpress.com/2015/07/01/if-im-so-smart-why-am-i-so-lonely/

rainforestmind.wordpress.com/2015/12/02/single-lonely-gifted/

welcometothedeepend.com: Stephanie Tolan, writer of young adult fiction and speaker on gifted topics

Chapter Six: School Daze
Books

The Boy Who Played With Fusion: Extreme Science, Extreme Parenting, And How To Make A Star, Tom Clynes

Colleges that Change Lives, Loren Pope

Cool Colleges: For the Hyper-Intelligent, Self-Directed, Late Blooming, and Just Plain Different, Donald Asher

Educating Your Gifted Child: How One Public School Teacher Embraced Homeschooling, Celi Trepanier

Geeks: How Two Lost Boys Rode the Internet out of Idaho, Jon Katz

Gifted Grownups, Marylou Streznewski

Giftedness 101, Linda Silverman

If This is a Gift, Can I Send it Back? Surviving in the Land of the Gifted and Twice Exceptional, Jen Merrill

How to Work and Homeschool: Practical Advice, Tips, and Strategies from Parents, Pamela Price

Smart Girls in the 21ˢᵗ Century: Understanding Talented Girls and Women, Barbara Kerr and Robyn McKay

Online

2enewsletter.com: Helping 2e children, for parents and educators

freespirit.com: Publisher of educational materials, including curriculum for gifted children

giftedhomeschoolers.org: GHF, dedicated to support for families of gifted/2e kids and publisher of books on giftedness, including this book

hoagiesgifted.org: Resource for all things gifted, including blogs by parents and professionals

Innovativelearningconference.org: The Nueva School's conference on innovation in education

NAGC.org: National Association for Gifted Children

sengifted.org: Supporting the Emotional Needs of the Gifted

prufrock.com: Publisher specializing in gifted educational materials for teachers

rainforestmind.wordpress.com/2015/01/21/gifted-adults-school-experiences/

rainforestmind.wordpress.com/2015/09/03/tips-for-teachers-and-parents-of-gifted-kids/

Chapter Seven: Authenticity and Creativity and Spirituality, Oh My!
Books

The Artist's Way, Julia Cameron

Cosmos, Carl Sagan

Dreaming the Soul Back Home, Robert Moss

Full Catastrophe Living: Using the Wisdom of Your Body and Mind to Face Stress, Pain, and Illness, Jon Kabat-Zinn

Letters to a Medicine Man: An Apprenticeship in Spiritual Intelligence, Barbara Kerr and John McAlister

Life's Companion: Journal Writing as Spiritual Quest, Christina Baldwin

Living Buddha, Living Christ, Thich Nhat Hanh

My Story as Told by Water, David James Duncan

Radical Acceptance: Embracing Your Life with the Heart of a Buddha, Tara Brach

Riding the Windhorse: Spiritual Intelligence and the Growth of the Self, Kathleen Noble

Religion for Atheists, Alain de Botton

Running the Long Race in Gifted Education, Joy M. Scott-Carrol and Anthony Sparks, eds.

Spells of Mending, Anne Allanketner

Toward a Psychology of Awakening: Buddhism, Psychotherapy and the Path of Personal and Spiritual Transformation, John Welwood

Untie the Strong Woman: Blessed Mother's Immaculate Love for the Wild Soul, Clarissa Pinkola Estes

Using Jewish Spiritual Wisdom to Become More Present, Centered, and Available for Life, Leonard Felder

The War of Art, Steven Pressfield

Wonders of the Universe, Brian Cox

Online

brainpickings.org/2013/12/20/carl-sagan-varieties-of-scientific-experience/: Carl Sagan's thoughts of science and religion

brainpickings.org/2014/09/15/sam-harris-waking-up-spirituality/: Maria Popova's collection of links to articles on science and spirit

brenebrown.com: Brene Brown, researcher, storyteller

cac.org/richardrohr: Center for Action and Contemplation, Richard Rohr

davidjamesduncan.com: David Duncan, writer, activist

davidwhyte.com: David Whyte, poet, visionary

haydenplanetarium.org/tyson/: Neil deGrasse Tyson, astrophysicist

jeanhouston.org: Jean Houston, scholar, philosopher, visionary, author

mayaangelou.com/books/: Maya Angelou, writer, poet, philosopher

patriciagatto-walden.com: Patricia Gatto-Walden psychologist specializing in giftedness and spirituality

ted.com/talks/alain_de_botton_atheism_2_0

Chapter Eight: Stop the Deforestation
Books

Bright Adults: Uniqueness and Belonging across the Lifespan, Ellen Fiedler

Bright, Talented, & Black: A Guide for Families of African American Gifted Learners, Joy
	Davis
A Parent's Guide to Gifted Teens: Living with Intense and Creative Adolescents, Lisa Rivero
The Power of Your Child's Imagination, Charlotte Reznick
Raising Your Spirited Child, Mary S. Kurcinka
Smart Boys: Talent, Manhood, and the Search for Meaning, Barbara Kerr and Sanford Cohn
Smart Girls in the 21st Century: Understanding Talented Girls and Women, Barbara Kerr and
	Robyn McKay
The Social and Emotional Development of Gifted Children: What Do We Know?, Maureen
	Neihart, et al
And Still We Rise: The Trials and Triumphs of Twelve Gifted Inner-City Kids, Miles Corwin
When Gifted Kids Don't Have All the Answers, Jim Delisle and Judy Galbraith

Online

"**Gifted Adults: A Systematic Review and Analysis of the Literature,**" Anne
	Rinn, James Bishop (*Gifted Child Quarterly*, Vol 59 (4)),
	http://gcq.sagepub.com/content/59/4/213.abstract
giftedhomeschoolers.org: GHF, dedicated to support for families of gifted/2e kids
	and publisher of books on giftedness, blogs by parents and professionals
hoagiesgifted.org: Resource for all things gifted, including blogs by parents and
	professionals
imageryforkids.com: Dr. Charlotte Reznick, psychologist
NAGC.org: National Association for Gifted Children
sengifted.org: Supporting the Emotional Needs of the Gifted

Endnotes

1. Diane Ackerman, *A Natural History of the Senses* (New York: Vintage, 1991).

2. Stephanie Tolan and Michael M. Piechowski, "Giftedness Lessons from Leeuwenhook," eds. Christine S. Neville, Michael M. Piechowski, and Stephanie Tolan, eds., *Off the Charts: Asynchrony and the Gifted Child* (Unionville, NY: Royal Fireworks Press, 2013), 1-8.

3. Scott Barry Kaufman, *Ungifted: Intelligence Redefined* (New York: Basic Books, 2015).
    David Shenk, *The Genius in All of Us: New Insights Into Genetics, Talent, and IQ* (New York: Doubleday, 2010).
    Linda Silverman, *Giftedness 101* (New York: Springer Publishing Company, 2013).

4. Mary-Elaine Jacobsen, *The Gifted Adult: A Revolutionary Guide for Liberating Everyday Genius.* (New York: Ballantine, 1999).

5. Mary-Elaine Jacobsen, "Encountering the Gifted Self Again, for the First Time," *Advanced Development,* vol. 8 (1999): 9-29.

6. Barbara A. Kerr and S. J. Cohn, *Smart Boys: Giftedness, Manhood, and the Search for Meaning.* (Scottsdale, AZ: Great Potential Press, 2001).
    Stephanie Tolan (1994). "Discovering the Gifted Ex-Child," accessed November 8, 2011. sengifted.org/archives/articles/discovering-the-gifted-ex-child.

7. James Webb, et al., *Misdiagnosis and Dual Diagnoses of Gifted Children and Adults,* (Scottsdale, AZ: Great Potential Press, 2005).

8. Susan Daniels and Michael Piechowski, eds., *Living with Intensity* (Scottsdale, AZ: Great Potential Press, 2009).

9. Elaine Aron, *The Highly Sensitive Person* (New York: Broadway, 1996).

10. Linda Silverman, *Counseling the Gifted and Talented* (Denver, CO: Love Publishing Company, 1993), 13.

11. Daniels and Piechowski, eds., Living with Intensity.
James Webb, *Searching for Meaning: Idealism, Bright Minds, Disillusionment and Hope.* (Tucson, AZ: Great Potential Press, 2013).

12. Karen Nelson, "Dabrowski's Theory of Positive Disintegration," *Advanced Development*, vol. 1 (1989): 47.

13. Jacobsen, "Encountering the Gifted Self Again, for the First Time," 9-29.

14. American Academy of Achievement, accessed September 23, 2012. achievement.org/autodoc/page/tan0int-1.

15. Annemarie Roeper, "Gifted Adults: Their Characteristics and Emotions," *Advanced Development*, vol. 3 (1991): 27.

16. Kathleen Noble, *Riding the Windhorse: Spiritual Intelligence and the Growth of the Self* (New Jersey: Hampton Press, 2001).
Barbara A. Kerr and John McAlister, *Letters to the Medicine Man: An Apprenticeship in Spiritual Intelligence* (New Jersey: Hampton Press, 2002).

17. Stephanie Tolan, "Imagination to Intuition: The Journey of a Rationalist into Realms of Magic and Spirit," *Advanced Development*, vol. 10 (2006): 45-57.

18. Andrew Boyd, *Daily Afflictions: The Agony of Being Connected to Everything in the Universe* (New York: W. W. Norton & Company, 2002).

19. Deborah Ruf, "If You're So Smart, Why Do You Need Counseling?" *Advanced Development*, vol. 8 (1999): 63-75.

20. Jacobsen, "Encountering the Gifted Self Again, for the First Time," 22-23.

21. Charles Eisenstein, *Sacred Economics: Money, Gift and Society in the Age of Transition* (Berkeley, CA: North Atlantic Books, 2011), 89.

22. Webb, et al., *Misdiagnosis and Dual Diagnoses of Gifted Children and Adults.*

23. Patty Gatto-Walden, "The Heart of the Matter: Complexities of the Highly Gifted Self," in *Off the Charts: Asynchrony and the Gifted Child*, eds. Christine S. Neville, Michael M. Piechowski, and Stephanie Tolan (Unionville, NY: Royal Fireworks Press, 2013), 158-82.

24. James Webb, *Searching for Meaning: Idealism, Bright Minds, Disillusionment and Hope* (Tucson, AZ: Great Potential Press, 2013).

25. Charles Eisenstein, "Naivete, and the Light in Their Eyes," *Charles Eisenstein,* accessed August 6, 2012. http://charleseisenstein.net/naivete-and-the-light-in-their-eyes/.

26. Eisenstein, "Naivete, and the Light in Their Eyes."

27. Bill Plotkin, *Soulcraft: Crossing into the Mysteries of Nature and Psyche* (Novato, CA: New World Library, 2003), 13.

28. Josh Fox, *Gasland*, 2010. gaslandthemovie.com.

29. Robert Goldman and Stephen Papson, *Nike Culture: The Sign of the Swoosh* (New York: SAGE Publications Ltd., 1998), 49.

30. Jane Burka and Lenora Yuen, *Procrastination: Why You Do It, What to do About it NOW* (Cambridge, MA: Perseus Books Group, 2008).

31. Roeper, "Gifted Adults," 21-34.

32. Daniels and Piechowski, eds., *Living with Intensity.*

33. Burka and Yuen, *Procrastination*, 136.

34. Diane Ackerman, *An Alchemy of Mind: The Marvel and Mystery of the Brain,* (New York: Scribner, 2004), 161.

35. Lee Anne Bell, "The Gifted Woman as Impostor," *Advanced Development*, vol 2 (1990): 55-64.

36. Joe Langford and Pauline Rose Clance, "The Impostor Phenomenon: Recent Research Findings Regarding Dynamics, Personality and Family Patterns and Their Implications for Treatment," *Psychotherapy*, vol. 30(3) (1993): 495-500.

37. Shenk, *The Genius in All of Us,* 29.

38. Carol Dweck, *Mindset: The New Psychology of Success* (New York: Random House, 2006).

39. Salvatore Mendaglio PhD and Jean Sunde Peterson PhD, *Models of Counseling: Gifted Children, Adolescents, and Young Adults* (Waco, TX: Prufrock Press, 2007), 240-241.

40. Burka and Yuen, *Procrastination,* 39.

41. Steven Pressfield, *The War of Art: Break Through the Blocks and Win Your Inner Creative Battles* (New York: Black Irish Entertainment, 2002), 143-144.

42. Bill Plotkin, *Soulcraft: Crossing into the Mysteries of Nature and Psyche* (Novato, CA: New World Library, 2003), 9-10.

43. Daniels and Piechowski, eds., *Living with Intensity.*

44. Silverman, *Giftedness 101.*

45. Roeper, "Gifted Adults," 21-34.

46. Shenk, *The Genius in All of Us,* 55.

47. Linda Silverman, "Through the Lens of Giftedness," *Roeper Review,* vol. 20(3), (1988): 206.

48. Jacobsen, "Encountering the Gifted Self Again, for the First Time," 21.

49. Edward M. Hallowell and John J. Ratey, *Delivered from Distraction* (New York: Ballantine, 2005).

50. Steve Jobs, Stanford Commencement Address 2005. https://www.ted.com/talks/steve_jobs_how_to_live_before_you_die

51. Silverman, *Counseling the Gifted and Talented,* 220-1

52. Barbara Sher, *Refuse to Choose! A Revolutionary Program for Doing Everything that You Love* (Emmaus, PA: Rodale, 2006).

53. Roeper, "Gifted Adults," 31-32.

54. Margaret Lobenstein, *The Renaissance Soul: How to Make Your Passions Your Life* (New York, Broadway, 2006), 2.

55. Sher, *Refuse to Choose,* 28.

56. Donald Antrim, "The Pancake Supper," *The New Yorker,* December 27, 1999, 100-109 and January 3, 2000, 104.

57. Edward Carr, "The Last Days of the Polymath," Autumn 2009, accessed August 27, 2013. http://moreintelligentlife.com/content/edward-carr/last-days-polymath.

58. Andrew Solomon, *Far from the Tree: Parents, Children and the Search for Identity* (New York: Scribner, 2013).

59. Crystal McCrary and Nathan Hale Williams, *Inspiration: Profiles of Black Women Changing our World* (New York: Abrams, 2012), 104.

60. Maureen Neihart Psy.D. and Steven Pfeiffer Ph.D, *The Social and Emotional Development of Gifted Children: What Do We Know?* (Waco, TX: Prufrock Press, 2002).

61. Linda Silverman, "Asynchronous Development," eds. Maureen Neihart Psy.D. and Steven Pfeiffer Ph.D, *The Social and Emotional Development of Gifted Children: What Do We Know?* (Waco, TX: Prufrock Press, 2002), 31-37.
Ellen Fiedler, "You Don't Outgrow It! Giftedness Across the Lifespan, "in *Off the Charts: Asynchrony and the Gifted Child*, eds. Christine S. Neville, Michael M. Piechowski, and Stephanie Tolan (Unionville, NY: Royal Fireworks Press, 2013), 183-210.

62. Marylou Streznewski, *Gifted Grown-ups: The Mixed Blessings of Extraordinary Potential* (New York: Wiley & Sons, 1999).
Lois Kelly and Carmen Medina, *Rebels at Work* (Sebastopol: O'Reilly, 2015).

63. Deidre V. Lovecky, "Warts and Rainbows: Issues in the Psychotherapy of the Gifted," *Advanced Development*, vol. 2 (1990): 65-83.

64. Tolan, " Discovering the Gifted Ex-Child," 6.

65. Jacobsen, "Encountering the Gifted Self Again, for the First Time," 18.

66. McCrary and Williams, *Inspiration*.

67. Ellen D. Fielder, *Bright Adults: Uniqueness and Belonging across the Lifespan* (Tucson, AZ: Great Potential Press, 2015), 176-7.

68. Pressfield, *The War of Art*.

69. Tom Clynes, *The Boy Who Played with Fusion: Extreme Science, Extreme Parenting, and How to Make a Star* (New York: Eamon Dolan/Houghton Mifflin Harcourt, 2015), 153.

70. Daniels and Piechowski, eds., *Living with Intensity*, 170-171.

71. Jacobsen, "Encountering the Gifted Self Again, for the First Time," 20.

72. Streznewski, *Gifted Grown-ups*.

73. Annemarie Roeper, *The "I" of the Beholder: A Guided Journey to the Essence of a Child*. (Scottsdale, AZ: Great Potential Press, 2007), 78.

74. Emily Graslie, "Did you like high school growing up? or did just ignore it and do your own thing," ehmeegee, *Tumblr*, accessed December 12, 2013. http://ehmeegee.tumblr.com/post/69441312697/did-you-like-high-school-growing-up-or-did-just-ignore#notes.

75. Streznewski, *Gifted Grown-ups*, 81.

76. Ackerman, *An Alchemy of Mind*, 161.

77. American Academy of Achievement, accessed September 23, 2012. achievement.org/autodoc/page/mol0int-1.

78. Karen B. Rogers, "Effects of Acceleration on Gifted Learners," eds. Maureen Neihart Psy.D. and Steven Pfeiffer Ph.D, *The Social and Emotional Development of Gifted Children: What Do We Know?* (Waco, TX: Prufrock Press, 2002), 3-12.

79. Ann Druyan and Carl Sagan, *The Demon-Haunted World: Science as a Candle in the Dark* (New York: Ballantine Books, 1997).

80. Bell, "The Gifted Woman as Impostor," 55-64.

81. Silverman, *Giftedness 101*.

82 Francine Shapiro, *Getting Past Your Past: Take Control of Your Life with Self-help Techniques from EMDR Therapy* (New York: Rodale, 2012).

83. Justin Kruger and David Dunning, "Unskilled and Unaware of It: How Difficulties in Recognizing One's Own Incompetence Lead to Inflated Self-Assessments," Journal of Personality and Social Psychology, vol. 77(6): 1121-34.

84. "Pearl S. Buck>Quote>Quotable Quotes," goodreads.com/quotes/31946-the-truly-creative-mind-in-any-field-is-no-more.

85. Pressfield, *The War of Art*, 146.

86. Aron, *The Highly Sensitive Person*.

87. Jane Piirto, *Talented Children and Adults* (Waco, TX: Prufrock, 2007), 412.

88. Annemarie Roeper, "Asynchrony and Sensitivity," in *Off the Charts: Asynchrony and the Gifted Child*, eds. Christine S. Neville, Michael M. Piechowski, and Stephanie Tolan (Unionville, NY: Royal Fireworks Press, 2013), 146-57.

89. Barbara Kerr and John McAlister, "Shamanic Journey: An Apprenticeship in Spiritual Intelligence," *Advanced Development*, vol. 9, (2000): 53.

90. Michael Piechowski, "Childhood Experiences and Spiritual Giftedness," *Advanced Development*, vol. 9 (2000): 70.

91. David Duncan, *God Laughs and Plays* (Great Barrington, MA: Triad Institute, 2006), xiv.

92. Roeper, *The "I" of the Beholder*, 126.

93. Aron, *The Highly Sensitive Person*, 224.

94. Aron, *The Highly Sensitive Person*, 209.

95. Patty Gatto-Walden, "Living One's Spirit Song: Transcendent Experiences in Counseling Gifted Adults," in *Off the Charts: Asynchrony and the Gifted Child*, edited by Christine S. Neville, Michael M. Piechowski, and Stephanie Tolan (Unionville, NY: Royal Fireworks Press, 2013), 203-23.

96. Gatto-Walden, "Living One's Spirit Song," 203-204.

97. Noble, *Riding the Windhorse*, 7.

98. Judith Blackstone, *Belonging Here: A Guide for the Spiritually Sensitive Person* (Boulder, CO: Sounds True, 2012), ix.

99. Kathleen Noble, "Spiritual Intelligence: A New Frame of Mind." *Advanced Development*, vol. 9 (2000): 26.

100. Noble, *Riding the Windhorse*, 122.

101. Animas Valley Institute, accessed April 23, 2016. http://www.animas.org/about-us/our-organization/what-we-do/.

102. Nicholas Kristof, "Obama and the War on Brains," *New York Times*, Nov. 9, 2008), accessed November 11, 2008. http://www.nytimes.com/2008/11/09/opinion/09kristof.html?em+&page%20 wanted+print&_r=0.

103. Burkhard Bilger, "Nerd Camp," *The New Yorker*, July 26, 2004, accessed March 20, 2013. http://eec.edc.org/cwis_docs/Miscellaneous/NY_Gifted.txt.

104. New York Times, Jan. 13, 2013.

105. mashable.com/2013/01/13.

106. Ronaldo Lemos, "My Email Exchange with Aaron Swartz Shows an Original Thinker," *Fast Company*, January 14, 2013, accessed January 14, 2013. http://www.fastcompany.com/3004769/my-email-exchange-aaron-swartz-shows-original-thinker.

107. Lemos, "My Email Exchange with Aaron Swartz Shows an Original Thinker."

108. Maureen Neihart, "The Impact of Giftedness on Psychological Well-Being," *Roeper Review*, 22(1), accessed March 24, 2013. www.sengifted.org/archives/articles/the-impact-of-giftedness-on-psychological-well-being.

Index

A

Abram, David, 155
achievement
    and definition of giftedness, xi–xii
    downplaying, 59–60, 79
    and existential depression, 38
    and impostor phenomenon, xvi, 141
    and intrinsic perfectionism, 62, 68
    praise for, 53, 54, 55, 64
    self-pressure for, xv, 43, 54, 55
Ackerman, Diane, ix, 56–57, 124
active listening, 96, 128–29, 148
activism, 129
    and existential depression, 41, 46, 47, 48
    and multipotentiality, 91
Adams, Kathleen, 78
ADD (attention deficit disorder)
    in addition to giftedness, 70, 71, 72, 76, 116, 137
    confused with giftedness, xv, 131–32
    treatment for, 74
additudemag.com, 137
alcohol, 35, 96–97
Allanketner, Anne, 161–64
all-or-nothing thinking, 79
Ally McBeal, 111
animals, 51. *See also* nature, responses to
animas.org, 50
Animas Valley Institute, 157
antidepressants, 30, 40, 74
Antrim, Donald, 88
anxiety
    and existential depression, 46
    and family of origin issues, 151–52
    and intensity, 22, 23–24, 26, 27
    and perfectionism, 58, 65
    and school experiences, 126, 127–28, 131
The Anxiety and Phobia Workbook (Bourne), 28
Argentine tango, 119
Aron, Elaine, 33, 145, 156

art. *See* visual art
Asher, Donald, 137
asking for help, 59, 73–74, 78–79. *See also* counseling
assumptions. *See* myths about gifted people
asynchrony, 105, 106–7, 123, 126
as You Like It (Shakespeare), 143
attention deficit disorder. *See* ADD
authenticity, 139–56
    case study: Beverly, 150–54
    case study: Eli, 149–50
    case study: Steven, 147–49
    and creativity, 143, 148, 149, 153–54
    and doubting one's own giftedness, 140–43
    and downplaying one's abilities, 140
    and multipotentiality, 44, 153
    and spirituality, 143–47, 150, 155, 156
author background, xiii–xiv
avaaz.org, 48

B

back-up singers, 111
"bad robot dance," 31, 32
Baldwin, Christina, 78
Banks, Rebecca, 76, 137
Be a Free Range Human (Cantwell), 101
beauty, appreciation for, 20–21, 43, 61. *See also* nature, responses to
Beck, Martha, 102
Belonging Here: A Guide to the Spiritually Sensitive Person (Blackstone), 97, 146, 156
Beth (case study), 44–47
Beverly (case study), 150–54
Bilger, Burkhard, 157
billmoyers.com, 49
Billy (case study), 22–27
bipolar disorder, 137
Blackstone, Judith, 97, 146, 156
boasting, 60

body awareness techniques, 24–25, 31–32
Boldt, Laurence, 103
boredom, 56, 78. *See also* intellectual
    stimulation, need for
boundaries, 26, 34, 35–36, 68, 113, 149
Bourne, Edmund, 28
Boyd, Andrew, 37, 41–42, 137
*The Boy Who Played With Fusion: Extreme Science,
    Extreme Parenting, And How To Make A
    Star* (Clynes), 137
brain plasticity, 58–59, 92
The Brain Scoop, 123–24
breathing techniques, 33, 48
Bright Not Broken (Kennedy & Banks), 76, 137
Brooks, Havi, 154
Buck, Pearl, 143
Buddhist practices, 48, 144
Burk, Connie, 50
Burka, Jane, 28, 56, 60, 80
Burroughs, William, 157

C

Cain, Susan, 73, 78, 118
Cantwell, Marianne, 101
career centers, 101
career choices
    and multipotentiality, 83–87, 89, 91, 93,
        101, 103
    and perfectionism, 69
    See also work environment
catastrophizing, 34, 79
childhood experiences
    intensity, 21
    loneliness, 105–7, 114
    spirituality, 144
    See also family of origin issues; school
        experiences
children. *See* parenting
Chodron, Pema, 48
Clynes, Tom, 121, 137
collaboration, 85, 107
college
    choosing, 47, 137
    and existential depression, 47
    and multipotentiality, 81
    and perfectionism, 58, 65, 67–68, 70, 71–
        72
    and school experiences, 125
Colleges That Change Lives (Pope), 47, 137
Colvin, Geoff, 58–59
compliments, 117
consulting, 69, 86
contradictory fears, xvi, 49–50
Cool Colleges (Asher), 137
counseling
    and authenticity, 142, 155–56
    need for, x
    and parenting, 35

and perfectionism, 78–79
    and sensitivity, 128, 156
    See also specific modalities
couples counseling, 119
creativity
    and authenticity, 143, 148, 149, 153–54
    and multipotentiality, 94, 96
    See also visual art
Cross, Tracy, 121
"Crystalline Structures" (Allanketner), 161–64
Cuddy, Amy, 79, 102

D

Dabrowski, Kazimierz, 19–20
*Daily Afflictions: The Agony of Being Connected to
    Everything in the Universe* (Boyd), 137
Dalai Lama, 156
dance, 119
decision-making, xv, 87–88, 103
depression
    and intensity, 27, 28
    medication for, 30, 40, 74
    and school experiences, 131
    See also existential depression
despair, 48. *See also* existential depression
dialogues, inner, 30, 78, 154
Diane (case study), 70–75
"Discovering the Gifted Ex-Child" (Tolan), 108
distraction as strategy, 26, 50
divergent thinking, 23, 56–57, 87–88, 103
"Diving Into the Wreck" (Rich), 142
Djerassi, Carl, 93
Dolgen, Ellen, 36
doubting one's own giftedness, xvi, 66
    and authenticity, 140–43
    and ease of learning, 92–93
    and intensity, 20, 23, 28
    and loneliness, 112
    and multipotentiality, 98
    and school experiences, 126, 129, 130
downplaying one's abilities, 59–60, 65, 73, 79,
    140, 151
drive to understand. *See* learning, love of
dumbing down. *See* downplaying one's abilities
Duncan, David James, 144–45
Dunning, David, 142
Dweck, Carol, 58, 59, 77–78, 92
dysfunctional families. *See* family of origin
    issues

E

Eden, Donna, 36
Edison, Thomas, 77
Einstein, Albert, 123
Eisenstein, Charles, 38, 39, 48
EMDR, 112

emotions
    and gender, 17, 95
    and intensity, 17, 23, 25
    See also empathy; sensitivity
empathy, xv, 21, 23, 26, 28. *See also* existential
    depression; intensity; sensitivity
empoweryou.com, 103
*Energy Medicine: Balancing Your Body's Energies for
    Optimal Health, Joy and Vitality* (Eden), 36
entelechy, 144
exercise, 33. *See also* movement
existential depression, xvi, 37–51, 73
    case study: Beth, 44–47
    case study: Gwen, 40–44
    and idealism, 39–40
    and school experiences, 133
    strategies for, 48–51
extraversion, 65, 111, 117
extrinsic perfectionism, 53–55

F

failure, fear of, 20, 63, 77
family of origin issues
    and anxiety, 151–52
    and authenticity, 148, 150, 151–52
    and doubting one's own giftedness, 141–
        42
    and dumbing down, 140
    and existential depression, 40, 42–43, 45
    grieving, 32, 44
    and inner child work, 96, 148–49, 153
    and intensity, 18–19, 27
    and loneliness, 111, 112
    and perfectionism, 43, 54, 64, 66–67, 68,
        73, 78
    and post-traumatic stress disorder, 28
    psychodynamic model for, 29–30
    and relationships, 95–96
fears
    contradictory, xvi, 49–50
    of failure, 20, 63, 77
    and loneliness, 118
    of success, 59–61, 73, 79
Fiedler, Ellen, 110
Flatow, Ira, 101
fluentself.com, 154
4-7-8 technique, 33
freethechildren.org, 48
friendships. *See* loneliness; relationships
Frost, Seena, 155

G

Gatto-Walden, Patricia, 39, 145
*Geeks: How Two Lost Boys Rode the Internet out of
    Idaho* (Katz), 138
"geek" term, 138

gender, 17, 95
The Genius is All of Us (Shenk), 58
The Gifted Adult (Jacobsen), 37–38
giftedhomeschoolers.org, 137–38
giftedness
    defined, xi–xii
    discomfort with label, xvi, 132, 136
    See also rainforest mind
Gina (case study), 64–70
Glass, Ira, 101
Golden, Thelma, 105–6
Goodall, Jane, 49
Gottman, John, 119
Graslie, Emilie, 123–24
gratitude, 43, 78
Greenspan, Miriam, 35
grief
    and family of origin issues, 32, 44
    and multipotentiality, 87
growth mindset, 58, 77–78
guided imagery, 96, 148–49, 150, 152–53
guilt, 48–49. *See also* existential depression
Gwen (case study), 40–44

H

Hallowell, Edward M., 74
Healing Through the Dark Emotions (Greenspan),
    35
healthjourneys.com, 35
The HeartMath Solution, 35
help, asking for, 59, 73–74, 78–79. *See also*
    counseling
helping. *See* service, desire for
Hendrix, Harville, 119
hiding one's abilities. *See* downplaying one's
    abilities
The Highly Sensitive Person (Aron), 33, 156
high standards, 24, 61, 62, 68, 76, 107. *See also*
    perfectionism
hormones, 36
Houston, Jean, 156
humor, 137

I

idealism, 28–29, 39–40, 61, 107
imageryforkids.com, 102
imagination, xvi, 18
"I" messages, 148
immersion learning, 91
impostor phenomenon, xvi, 57–58, 141
Ingerman, Sandra, 36, 156
inner child work, 96, 148–49, 153
inner dialogues, 30, 78, 154
innovativelearningconference.org, 136
Institute of Noetic Sciences, 156
intellectual stimulation, need for, xvi

and intrinsic perfectionism, 63–64, 65
and parenting, 102
and procrastination, 56, 78
and school experiences, 122, 132, 133, 136
See also learning, love of
intelligence as changeable, 58–59, 92
intensity, 17–36
    and appreciation for beauty, 20–21
    case study: Billy, 22–27
    case study: Janice, 27–32
    and empathy, 21, 23, 26, 28
    and existential depression, 42
    overexcitabilities, 19
    strategies for, 33–36
    Theory of Positive Disintegration, 19–20
    See also speed
Internal Family Systems theory, 30, 154
intrinsic perfectionism, 61–64, 68, 76, 134
introspection, 20
introversion, 73, 78, 118
intuition, 21, 36. *See also* empathy; psychic
    experiences
The I of the Beholder (Roeper), 123
isolation. *See* loneliness

J

Jacobsen, Mary-Elaine, 17, 20, 37–38, 63, 109,
    122
janegoodall.org, 49
Janice (case study), 27–32
jealousy, 59, 151
Jobs, Steve, 80
Johnson, Susan, 119
Jordan, Michael, 53
journaling
    inner dialogues, 78, 154
    and intensity, 33
    and loneliness, 112, 118
    and multipotentiality, 102
    and parenting, 35
    and perfectionism, 78
Jung, Carl, 149

K

Katz, Jon, 138
Kelly, Lois, 103
Kennedy, Diane, 76, 137
Kerr, Barbara, 59, 144, 156
Kristof, Nicholas, 157
Kruger, Justin, 142
Kurcinka, Mary, 102

L

Lamott, Anne, 155
learning, ease of

and authenticity, 141
and doubting one's own giftedness, 92–93
and perfectionism, 53, 54–55, 57, 70
taking on challenges, 26, 77–78, 92–93
See also perfectionism
learning, love of
    and intensity, 19–20, 25–26
    and multipotentiality, 82, 90, 91
    and school experiences, 122
learning disabilities, 137
learning style, 72, 91, 132
Letters to the Medicine Man (Kerr), 156
Levine, Peter, 31
Lewis, C. S., 156
life purpose, 50, 144
Limitless, 66
Lipsky, Laura Van Dernoot, 50
Lobenstein, Margaret, 83, 101
loneliness, 105–19, 157–58
    and asynchrony, 105, 106–7
    case study: Ruth, 114–16
    case study: Whitney, 111–14
    childhood experiences, 105–7
    and existential depression, 42, 45–46
    and perfectionism, 64, 65
    and relationships, 110–11, 112–13, 115–16,
        117
    and school experiences, 45–46, 70, 106,
        114, 124–25, 132, 151
    strategies for, 117–19
    in work environment, 107–8, 113

M

Macy, Joanna, 41, 48
marijuana, 35, 96–97
marthabeck.com, 102
meaning, drive towards, 39, 139, 143. *See also*
    authenticity; existential depression;
    spirituality
medication
    for ADD, 71, 72, 74
    antidepressants, 30, 40, 74
    and existential depression, 40
    and sensitivity, 18
Medina, Carmen, 103
meditation, 48, 149, 150. *See also* guided
    imagery; spirituality; visualization
Melanie (case study), 98–100
melatonin, 33
menopause, 36
methodology, xii–xiii
mindfulness practices, 144
Mindset (Dweck), 77–78
mistakes, 77
Molina, Mario, 125
The Mood Cure (Ross), 35
*The More Beautiful World Our Hearts Know is
    Possible* (Eisenstein), 48

Moss, Robert, 156
movement, 31–32, 33, 34, 66
Moyers, Bill, 49
multipotentiality, 81–103
    and authenticity, 44, 153
    and career choices, 83–87, 89, 91, 93, 101,
        103
    case study: Melanie, 98–100
    case study: Rebecca, 89–93
    case study: Richard, 94–97
    and decision-making, 87–88
    and love of learning, 82, 90, 91
    strategies for, 101–3
    and taking on challenges, 26
mundane tasks, 56, 62, 63, 72, 76, 133
music, and sleep, 33
Myss, Caroline, 36
myths about gifted people
    school success, 57, 121–22
    self-confidence, 20
    self-sufficiency, x, 64, 109
    See also others' reactions

N

NAGC.org, 138
"Naiveté, and the Light in their Eyes"
    (Eisenstein), 39
National Organization for Gifted Children
    (NAGC), 138
nature, responses to
    and existential depression, 41, 42
    and intensity, 19, 22
    and loneliness, 118
    and school experiences, 134
    and spirituality, xv, 144–45, 155
    as strategy for intensity, 33
Nature and the Human Soul (Plotkin), 155
Nauta, Noks, 103
negative thinking, 51. *See also* self-criticism
Neilhart, Maureen, 159
neurofeedback, 71, 74
Noble, Kathleen, 146, 147, 155
noetic.org, 36, 156
noksnauta.nl, 103
nonviolent communication, 96
nutrition, 33, 66

O

obsession, 62, 63
obsessive-compulsive disorder (OCD), xv, 137
OCD (obsessive-compulsive disorder), xv, 137
OEs (overexcitabilities), 19
Orloff, Judith, 36
others' reactions
    to achievement, 54
    to existential depression, 38–39, 41, 42

to high functioning, 28–29
    to intensity, 18–19, 20, 42
    to intrinsic perfectionism, 62, 65
    jealousy, 59, 151
    to multipotentiality, 82–83, 91
    and school experiences, 123
    in work environment, 107–8
    See also myths about gifted people
overexcitabilities (OEs), 19

P

"The Pancake Breakfast" (Antrim), 88
parenting
    and authenticity, 147–48, 149
    and intensity, 34–35
    and loneliness, 114
    and multipotentiality, 88–89, 98, 99–100,
        102
    and school experiences, 137–38
parents. *See* family of origin issues
pemachodronfoundation.org, 48
Perel, Esther, 119
perfectionism, 53–80
    case study: Diane, 70–75
    case study: Gina, 64–70
    and decision-making, 103
    and divergent thinking, 56–57
    and ease of learning, 53, 54–55, 57, 70
    and existential depression, 38
    extrinsic, 53–55
    and family of origin issues, 43, 54, 64, 66–
        67, 68, 73, 78
    and fear of success, 59–61, 73
    and growth mindset, 58–59, 77–78
    and impostor phenomenon, 57–58
    and intensity, 24, 30–31
    intrinsic, 61–64, 68, 76, 134
    and procrastination, 54, 55–56, 65, 66
    and school experiences, 54, 55, 58, 61, 70,
        133
    strategies for, 76–80
    taking on challenges as strategy for, 26,
        77–78
physical touch, 51
Piechowski, Michael, 144
Piirto, Jane, 143–44
Plotkin, Bill, 40, 50, 61, 155, 156
podcasting, 101
Pope, Loren, 47, 137
post-traumatic stress disorder (PTSD), 28, 112
power animals, 33
practicing, and perfectionism, 55
praise, 53, 54, 55, 64, 70, 93
Presence (Cuddy), 79, 102
Pressfield, Steven, 60–61, 77, 110–11, 143
process, emphasis on, 77
procrastination, 30–31
    and need for intellectual stimulation, 56, 78

and perfectionism, 54, 55–56, 65, 66
   strategies for, 68, 80
Procrastination (Burka & Yuen), 28, 56, 60, 80
psychic experiences, 21, 36, 130, 145
psychodynamic model, 29–30
psychotherapy. *See* counseling
PTSD (post-traumatic stress disorder), 28, 112
The PTSD Sourcebook, 28
purpose, 50, 144
puttylike.com, 87, 101

Q

*Quiet: The Power of Introverts in a World That Can't
   Stop Talking* (Cain), 78, 118
quietrev.com, 118

R

rainforest mind
   defined, xi
   deforestation of, 157–59
   as matter of degree, xi, 21
   quiz for identifying, xv–xvi
Raising Your Spirited Child (Kurcinka), 35, 102
reading, 18–19, 109
Realization Process, 146
Rebecca (case study), 89–93
Rebels at Work (Medina & Kelly), 103
Refuse to Choose (Sher), 84, 102, 153
rejection. *See* loneliness
relationships
   active listening for, 96, 128–29, 148
   boundaries in, 26, 34, 35–36, 68, 113, 149
   caretaking in, 26, 34, 35–36, 45, 112
   and existential depression, 46–47
   and family of origin issues, 95–96
   and loneliness, 110–11, 112–13, 115–16,
      117
   and multipotentiality, 90, 92
   and perfectionism, 65, 68, 69, 76
   resources for, 119
   work collaboration, 85, 107
   See also family of origin issues; loneliness
religion. *See* spirituality
The Renaissance Soul (Lobenstine), 83, 101
Renaissance souls. *See* multipotentiality
resilience, 28–29, 112, 142
Reznick, Charlotte, 102
Rhimes, Shonda, 109
Rich, Adrienne, 142
Richard (case study), 94–97
*Riding the Windhorse: Spiritual Intelligence and the
   Growth of the Self* (Noble), 155
The River Why (Duncan), 144–45
Roach, Mary, 87, 103
Roeper, Annemarie, 20–21, 82, 123, 144, 145
Rosenberg, Marshall, 96

Ross, Julia, 35
rumination, 20, 34, 50, 82
Rushmore, 108
Ruth (case study), 114–16

S

Sacred Economics (Eisenstein), 38
Sagan, Carl, 139, 156
saving the world. *See* existential depression
scanners. *See* multipotentiality
school experiences, xv, 111, 121–38
   case study: Tom, 126–30
   case study: Will, 130–35
   and loneliness, 45–46, 70, 106, 114, 124–
      25, 132, 151
   and perfectionism, 54, 55, 58, 61, 70, 133
   and procrastination, 54, 56
   and sensitivity, 23, 25
   strategies for, 25, 47, 136–38
Schwartz, Richard, 30, 154
Science Friday, 101
The Secret Thoughts of Successful Women (Young),
   79
self-actualization, 63
self-care, 26, 36, 44, 99
self-criticism
   and family of origin issues, 29, 152
   and intensity, 20
   and loneliness, 106
   and school experiences, 122, 124
   strategies for, 51, 78
self-employment, 71, 85–86, 114–15
self-soothing techniques, 24–25, 26, 35, 36
self-talk, 46, 133–34
SENG (Supporting the Emotional Needs of
   the Gifted), 138
sensitivity, xv, 18, 98
   and anxiety, 28
   and authenticity, 149–50
   and counseling, 128, 156
   and decision-making, 88
   and existential depression, 41–42
   and others' reactions, 20
   protection strategies for, 33
   and school experiences, 23, 25
   and spirituality, 146
   See also emotions; intensity
service, desire for, 26, 49, 89, 90. *See also*
   empathy
Shakespeare, William, 143
shamanism, 36, 144
shame, 18–19, 42, 44. *See also* self-criticism
Shenk, David, 58–59, 63
Sher, Barbara, 83, 102, 153
shmirshky.com, 36
Silverman, Linda, 63, 81
skepticism, 24–25
sleep, 33, 46

small talk, 118
Solomon, Andrew, 105
somatic experiencing, 31. *See also* body
        awareness techniques
SoulCollage Evolving (Frost), 155
Soulcraft (Plotkin), 40
soundstrue.com, 36
speed, xvi, 107–8, 109, 115, 133. *See also*
        intensity
spirituality
        and authenticity, 143–47, 150, 155, 156
        and existential depression, 49
        and loneliness, 110–11
        and multipotentiality, 97
        and perfectionism, 69
        and responses to nature, xv, 144–45, 155
        strategies for, 155–56
Steven (case study), 147–49
stress reduction techniques, 33. *See also* self-
        soothing techniques
Streznewski, Marylou, 124
substance use, 96–97, 161–64
*The Subtle Self: Personal Growth and Spiritual
        Practice* (Blackstone), 156
success, fear of, 59–61, 73, 79
suicide, 158–59
The Survival Guide for Parents of Gifted Kids
        (Walker), 148
Swartz, Aaron, 158–59

T

TAG (Talented and Gifted) conferences, 138
taking breaks, 51
Tan, Amy, 20, 109
tango, 119
teaching, 90
TED.com, 50, 101
test-taking, 23, 126, 127–28
Theory of Positive Disintegration (TPD), 19–
        20
therapy. *See* counseling
thinking something is wrong with you, 18, 22,
        34, 118, 136
This American Life, 101
350.org, 41
Tolan, Stephanie, 21, 108
Tom (case study), 126–30
tonglen meditation, 48
"too much". *See* intensity
touch. *See* physical touch
TPD (Theory of Positive Disintegration), 19–
        20
trauma, 28, 29–30, 45, 50, 66, 67, 152. *See also*
        family of origin issues
*Trauma Stewardship: An Everyday Guide to Caring
        for Self While Caring for Others* (Lipsky &
        Burk), 50
twice-exceptionalities, 76, 137, 138. *See also*

ADD
2enewsletter.com, 137

V

visual art, 44, 112, 118, 134, 155
visualization, 48–49, 152, 153. *See also* guided
        imagery

W

Walker, Sally, 148
Wapnick, Emilie, 87
The War of Art (Pressfield), 60–61, 77
Watts, Alan, 156
Welwood, John, 119
Whitney (case study), 111–14
Wild Mind (Plotkin), 50
Will (case study), 130–35
wonder, 20–21
work environment
        loneliness in, 107–8, 113
        and multipotentiality, 82, 84–85, 103
        and perfectionism, 55
        See also career choices
writing, 23, 30–31
wrongness, feeling of, 18, 22, 34, 118, 136

Y

Young, Valerie, 79
Yuen, Lenora, 28, 56, 60, 80

Acknowledgments

I'm deeply grateful to all of the clients, students, and blog followers with whom I have worked over the years, who have shared their fears, vulnerabilities, and sensitive, compassionate hearts with me. I especially want to thank the dear clients who allowed me to tell their stories here.

I appreciate the meticulous conscientiousness of my editor, Sarah Wilson, and her equally diligent cohort at GHF Press, Corin Barsily Goodwin. I am so happy to be a part of an organization of folks dedicated to the welfare of children, their parents, and the planet.

And finally, I can't begin to name all of the friends, therapists, authors, healing arts practitioners, bloggers, and family members who have guided, loved and put up with me all of these years. Thank you.

About the Author

Paula Prober, MS, MEd, is a licensed counselor in private practice in Eugene, Oregon. Over the 30+ years she has worked with the gifted, she has been a teacher, consultant, adjunct instructor with the University of Oregon, and a guest presenter at Pacific University and Oregon State University. She has taught sessions on gifted adults and on parenting gifted children at conferences and webinars.

Presently, she is counseling gifted adults and youth and consulting with parents of gifted children. She has written articles on giftedness for the *Eugene Register-Guard*, the *Psychotherapy Networker*, *Advanced Development Journal* and the *Annals of the American Psychotherapy Association*. She blogs about gifted adults and parenting gifted children at rainforestmind.wordpress.com.